Workshop Management:
Method to Magic

✶✶

A Resource for Facilitators

by

Dorothy Strachan and Marian Pitters

ST Press
Ottawa
Canada

Copyright © 2003 by Dorothy Strachan and Marian Pitters. All rights reserved.

National Library of Canada Cataloguing in Publication Data

Strachan, Dorothy, 1947
      Workshop Management, method to magic: a resource for facilitators/Dorothy Strachan, Marian Pitters

(ST Press Facilitation Series)
Includes bibliographical references.
ISBN #0-9688036-1-X

      1. Workshops (Adult Education)–Handouts, manuals, etc.
I. Pitters, Marian, 1952- II. Title. III. Series.

AS6.S76 2003   658.3'124   C2003-903216-7

Production: Peter Ashley
Copy Edit: Ann Anderson
Design: David Farrar, Farrar Graphics
Printing: Lowe-Martin
Artwork: Albert Prisner
Research: Karen Metcalfe

For information about other ST Press resources, please contact us at the number below or by email, or visit our Web site at www.stpress.ca.

ST Press
31 Euclid Avenue
Ottawa, Ontario, Canada
K1S 2W2
1-613-730-1000
1-800-572-1564 (in Canada and USA)
stpress@cyberus.ca

Contents

Acknowledgements i
Preface iii
How to Use This Handbook v

Part I: Workshop Management That Works

    Introduction 3

Chapter 1 – Method to Magic 5
    Method and Magic 8
    Getting From Method To Magic 9
    Anti-Magic Workshop Management 10

Chapter 2 – A Diagnostic Framework 15
    Eight Categories 19

Chapter 3 – Decision Making 37
    A. Structure 40
    B. Process 49
    Conclusion 53

Part II: Tips, Tools and Templates

    Introduction 57

Chapter 4 – Participants 59
    A. Types of Participation 62
    B. Mix of Participants 68
    C. Number of Participants 75
    D. Observers 77
    E. Participant Database 81
    F. Participant Accessibility 85

Chapter 5 – Invitations 91
    A. Letters and Announcements 94
    B. International Requirements 119
    C. Challenging Situations 124

Chapter 6 – Logistics, Locations and Layouts 131
    A. Logistics 134
    B. Locations 157
    C. Layouts 162

Chapter 7 – Speakers 169
    A. Opening Remarks 172
    B. Presentations by Experts 187
    C. Panel Presentations 206
    D. Closing Remarks 210

Chapter 8 – Handouts 215
    A. Content 218
    B. Design 223
    C. Six Key Handouts 232

Chapter 9 – Feedback 241
    A. Getting Good Feedback 244
    B. Acting on Feedback 254

Further Reading 273

CD-ROM with Tools and Templates . . . . .see back cover

TOOLS AND TEMPLATES

Chapter 2 - A Diagnostic Framework
Template 2.1   Workshop Diagnostic Framework 31

Chapter 4 - Participants
Tool 4.1   What's Your Type? 67
Tool 4.2   Participant Mix 72
Tool 4.3   Do We Have the Right Participants? .73
Tool 4.4   Participant Matrix for a National Research Summit 74
Tool 4.5   Observers - Yes or No? 80
Tool 4.6   Database Checklist 83
Template 4.7   Participant Database Information .84
Template 4.8   Participant Accessibility Map 88

Chapter 5 - Invitations
Tool 5.1   Letters and Announcements: A Checklist 103
Tool 5.2   Sample First Paragraphs 105
Tool 5.3   Soliciting Feedback on a Draft Invitation 107
Tool 5.4   Invitation to a Network Planning Retreat 108
Template 5.5   Email Announcement and Questionnaire for an In-House Training Workshop .110
Template 5.6   Invitation to Participate in a Pre-Retreat Survey 111
Template 5.7   Invitation Requesting Participation in a Mandatory Workshop and Survey . . .112
Template 5.8   Advance Announcement: Open Invitation 114
Template 5.9   Written Announcement: Regional Workshop 115
Template 5.10 Short Form Advance Electronic Announcement for a National Conference . .116
Template 5.11 Long Form Electronic Announcement for a National Conference 117
Template 5.12 Request for Official Invitation 121
Template 5.13 Official Invitation 122
Template 5.14 Letter of Support 123
Tool 5.15   Paragraphs for Challenging Situations 125

Chapter 6 - Logistics, Locations and Layouts
Tool 6.1   Checklist: Session-Specific Logistics 140
Tool 6.2   Checklist: Mobile Office Logistics .143
Tool 6.3   Checklist: Technical and Audiovisual Logistics 147
Tool 6.4   Checklist: Personal Logistics Kit 150
Tool 6.5   Checklist: International and Cross-Cultural Logistics 152
Tool 6.6   Checklist: Travel Logistics 154
Tool 6.7   Site Visit Checklist 160
Tool 6.8   Room Layouts 165

Chapter 7 - Speakers

Template 7.1	Outline for Opening Remarks for a National Research Workshop	180
Template 7.2	Opening Remarks for a National Research Workshop	181
Tool 7.3	Outline for Opening Remarks for a Regional Sales Meeting	184
Template 7.4	Opening Remarks for a Regional Sales Meeting	185
Tool 7.5	Checklist for Managing Expert Speakers	192
Tool 7.6	Commercialism Policies	195
Tool 7.7	Sample Outline – Speaker's Manual	197
Tool 7.8	What Speakers Need to Know Before They Present	198
Tool 7.9	Outline for a Letter of Confirmation to Speakers	199
Template 7.10	Letter of Confirmation to Speakers	200
Tool 7.11	Outline for Final Pre-Workshop Letter to Expert Speakers	203
Template 7.12	Final Pre-Workshop Letter to Expert Speakers	204
Tool 7.13	Checklist for Conducting Panels	209
Tool 7.14	Outline for Closing Remarks	212
Template 7.15	Closing Remarks	213

Chapter 8 - Handouts

Tool 8.1	Possible Handouts: A Checklist	227
Template 8.2	Introductions	229
Template 8.3	Guidelines for Working Together	230
Template 8.4	Resources for Further Learning	231
Template 8.5	Glossary of Verbs	234
Template 8.6	What are mission and vision statements?	235
Template 8.7	Quotables: An Introductory Activity	237
Template 8.8	Participant Information Bank	238
Template 8.9	Program Information Bank	239
Template 8.10	Acronyms Made Easy: Terms and Organizations	240

Chapter 9 - Feedback

Tool 9.1	Areas for Feedback Checklist	247
Tool 9.2	Sample Questions for Information Areas	250
Tool 9.3	Designing a Feedback or Evaluation Instrument	253
Template 9.4	Interim Participant Feedback – A	255
Template 9.5	Interim Participant Feedback – B	256
Template 9.6	Interim Participant Feedback – C	257
Template 9.7	Interim Participant Feedback – D	258
Template 9.8	Day One Feedback Sheet	259
Template 9.9	End of Session Feedback – A	260
Template 9.10	End of Session Feedback – B	261

Template 9.11	Visioning Day Evaluation	262
Template 9.12	Feedback on the Meeting	263
Template 9.13	Feedback on Planning Workshop	265
Template 9.14	Conference Workshop Feedback Form	266
Template 9.15	Feedback – Perspectives on a Symposium	267
Template 9.16	Workshop Manager's Reflections on a Session	268
Template 9.17	Workshop Manager's Program Log – A	269
Template 9.18	Workshop Manager's Program Log – B	270
Template 9.19	Client Feedback	272

Acknowledgements

The following colleagues reviewed earlier versions of this manuscript. Their rich experience and insightful feedback contributed enormously to the quality of this publication.

Yvonne Appiah	Executive Director, Canadian Organization for Development through Education
Randy Brooks	Partner, WilsonBrooks, Organizational Development Practitioners
Joan MacKenzie Davies	Executive Director, Ontario Association of Social Workers
Pam Fitch	Massage Therapist and Trainer
Alex Gontar	Director of Distributed Learning, the Michener Institute for Applied Health Sciences
Dinny Holroyd	National Director, Volunteer and Staff Development, The Kidney Foundation of Canada
Michael Luke	Facilitator in private practice
Lyle Makosky	President, Interquest Consulting
Rose Mercier	Maverick Consulting
Jack Miller	Professor, Ontario Institute for Studies in Education, University of Toronto
Maureen Nyilis	Governor's Office of Employee Relations, New York State
Carol Richardson	Administrative Officer, Canadian Institutes of Health Research, Institute of Infection and Immunity
Mary Jane Sterne	Facilitator in private practice
Nancy Tushingham	Artistic Advisor

*Special thanks to **Susan Wheeler**, Editor of CMT (Charcot-Marie-Tooth) magazine, who advised us on considerations related to accessibility (Chapter 4) and who is an inspirational advocate and role model for people with disabilities.*

Preface

As professional facilitators, we spend a great deal of time thinking about what makes workshops successful. One thing we know for sure: great workshop experiences are unlikely without thoughtful session management.

Workshop management includes all the decisions made in relation to the diligent administration of a session, e.g., how participants are selected and invited, where a session is held, how presentations are aligned with the workshop objectives, how worksheets are used, what food is served, what types of reports are written, what questions are selected to solicit feedback. Over the years it has become increasingly obvious that decisions about these administrative factors can make a significant contribution to the quality of workshop outcomes and your enjoyment as a facilitator.

Method to Magic

We have also concluded that, whatever the situation, participants are happier and more productive when workshops are managed with both method and magic in mind. "Method" is what you do administratively to optimize the workshop experience for participants – it's about efficient and effective systems that serve the workshop's purpose. The "magic" part happens as a result of good method: it's found in the experience of participants as they work through the process. In exceptional workshops, the magic can result in transformational experiences for some participants.

Developing successful workshops is a bit like making a special dinner. First you decide who to invite and check to see if anyone has allergies or special dietary requirements. Then whoever is cooking decides on an appropriate menu, selecting courses that will complement one another; finds and prepares quality ingredients; sorts out the sequence and timing for what gets cooked first, second and for how long; decides on presentation details such as arrangement on the plate. Others help with cleaning the house, arranging the eating area, setting the table, putting out candles and napkins, suggesting who will sit where, anticipating drinks to be served. Finally, the cook turns to serving the meal.

In comparison to the preparation time, the actual eating doesn't take long, but happens in stages, with the dessert coming last. At some level the dinner guests are aware of the effort it has taken to prepare the event and their appreciation extends into the conversation. When these dinners work well, guests often describe their experience of the meal, the setting, the people, and the conversation as being magical.

Workshop management is similar in many ways. It takes considerable time and some thoughtful decision making to ensure that you have done the following: chosen the right people for a session; understood their backgrounds and special needs; selected an appropriate venue; invited engaging speakers; provided pre-workshop information; developed well-designed handouts; timed meals and breaks in the agenda so that there is a smooth flow from registration to evaluation. And it almost always takes more time to prepare for the workshop than it takes to participate in the session. When workshops work well, participants (like the guests at a well-organized dinner party) often describe the experience and how they worked with others as being magical. Participants feel valued and respected; the organization of the event appears to be seamless; and everyone involved is aware at some level of the effort that has gone into making the initiative a success.

Workshop Management for Facilitators

This book is for anyone who is responsible for organizing and implementing a workshop. This includes facilitators and managers, as well as teachers, trainers, community organizers, project leaders, lawyers, physicians, human resources professionals, association executives, mediators, negotiators, social workers and counsellors. This guide is not about managing large conferences – that is the work of professional meeting planners.

More and more work is getting done in group or team situations. People in organizations talk frequently about "workshopping" a task. This "how to" guide will reduce the amount of time and effort required for you to manage workshops efficiently and with flair. As with other resources in this series, the focus is on basic frameworks, practical and proven tips, adaptable tools and a wealth of time-saving templates, strategies and examples for you to customize to individual situations.

Dorothy Strachan and Marian Pitters

Ottawa, Canada

June, 2003

How to Use This Handbook

This handbook has two main parts.

Part I: Workshop Management That Works, describes core concepts in a systematic approach to organizing workshops:

>Chapter 1 – Method to Magic

>Chapter 2 – A Diagnostic Framework

>Chapter 3 – Decision Making.

Part II: Tips, Tools and Templates, includes ideas, strategies and sample outlines for acting on the results of the diagnosis and decisions in Part I:

>Chapter 4 – Participants

>Chapter 5 – Invitations

>Chapter 6 – Logistics, Locations and Layouts

>Chapter 7 – Speakers

>Chapter 8 – Handouts

>Chapter 9 – Feedback.

Helpful books, articles and other resources are listed at the end of the book. Electronic versions of templates are included on the enclosed CD-ROM (back cover) to enable quick customization.

Although chapters are designed to stand on their own, they are also interrelated. For example, the information on participants in Chapter 4 will have an impact on the location and room layout discussed in Chapter 6, and will also help determine the speakers you select based on guidelines in Chapter 7.

We know that the concepts, approaches, tips, tools and templates in this book work – we have enjoyed using and refining them for many years. Try them out and customize them to your situation. They will save you time and energy, prevent duplication, and bring method and magic into your workshops.

About Words

Words used frequently throughout this book are explained below.

Client The client is the person to whom the facilitator is accountable. The client may be a supervisor, director or administrator. She may be part of a planning committee, represent a Board of Directors, or be another contractor. We find it's best to have one person designated as the client for accountability and liaison purposes.

Sometimes you are both client and facilitator, e.g., if you are a team manager and you are facilitating an internal team development workshop in your company.

Facilitator A facilitator is someone who attends to group process. This may include professional facilitators as well as teachers, trainers, community organizers, project leaders, lawyers, physicians, human resources professionals, executives, mediators, negotiators, social workers, counsellors, journalists and managers. Many people do facilitation as a regular part of their work and yet don't think of themselves as professional facilitators - they are included in this definition.

Group Three or more people who want to accomplish something.

Group members Participants in a group process; "group members" is used interchangeably with "participants."

Participants People who participate in a process; "participants" is used interchangeably with "group members."

Plenary When all members of an assembly are present, e.g., when a number of small groups are together in a meeting of the whole group.

Process A structured group experience, usually designed to achieve a specific outcome. A process may happen in a variety of settings such as work sessions, workshops, meetings, conferences, roundtables.

Session A facilitated process that happens in a limited time period - a few hours, a day, a weekend, a week. May also be called a workshop, meeting or conference. The word "session" is used interchangeably with the word "workshop."

Tips Suggestions, key points, guiding principles based on experience and expertise.

Tools Handy checklists, outlines, approaches, short cuts and time savers - "what works" based on successful practice.

Template A pattern for constructing a customized approach.

Workshop A facilitated process with a specific purpose that happens in a limited time period – a few hours, a day, a weekend, a week. Workshops come with a wide variety of purposes and in many shapes and sizes. Some workshops are formal, institutionalized events such as orientation sessions for new employees, strategic planning retreats or team-development events; others are informal learning situations involving six to nine people meeting in a community hall; still others are educational sessions within a larger conference or an annual general meeting. Regardless of format, orientation or size, workshops actively involve individuals and groups in doing "work" that is focused on stated outcomes.

Workshop Management Workshop management is about the conscious and deliberate administrative decisions made in support of session outcomes. It includes participant selection, logistics, planning structures, location and room set-up, speaker alignment with workshop objectives, worksheets and handouts, and feedback. The word "administration" is used interchangeably with the word "management." Workshop management is usually undertaken by a facilitator, members of an organizing committee and/or someone designated for this purpose.

Please note that gender-specific personal pronouns are used throughout the text to avoid using the cumbersome his/her or he/she constructions.

Unreferenced quotations in italics reflect the experiences of the authors and workshop participants. Some remarks are from workshop evaluation forms, others from taped sessions or informal conversations with colleagues and participants.

Part I

Workshop Management That Works

Introduction

The chapters in Part I explore the basics of effective workshop management.

Chapter 1 – Method to Magic, describes a systematic approach to workshop management. It explores two key elements – method and magic – and how these elements can enable participants' productivity and enjoyment. Six anti-magic styles are introduced, along with considerations for addressing them.

Chapter 2 – A Diagnostic Framework, is a step-by-step approach to the first part of method: scoping a workshop and diagnosing related challenges and opportunities. The diagnostic framework has eight categories:

1. Why this Workshop
2. Workshop Coordinates
3. Type of Session
4. Roles, Responsibilities and Accountability
5. Participants
6. Context
7. Pre-meeting Package
8. Best Scenario.

This chapter also describes 15 types of workshops, their unique features, and implications for managing them successfully.

Chapter 3 – Decision Making, focuses on the second part of method: decision making that generates magic for participants and clients. Once you have used the Diagnostic Framework in Chapter 2 to outline session specifications and diagnose the management challenges, the next step is to make decisions that reflect the conclusions in your diagnosis. Two aspects of decision making are explored in this chapter: structure and process.

Chapter 1

Method to Magic

★★★★★★★★★★★★★★★★★★★★★★★★

★★★★★★★★★★★★★★★★★★★★★★★★

Method to Magic

From a facilitator's perspective, the best workshops happen when you get the right blend of facilitation and management in service of the session purpose, participants and expected outcomes. The facilitator is ultimately accountable for ensuring that the workshop administration supports both the group process and the agenda. Whether you are assisted by a professional meeting manager or are organizing a session yourself, the buck stops with you.

Where a workshop is held, who is invited, how speakers are selected and briefed, the configuration of the room, content and format of the pre-session package, how the report is written - each of these management decisions has considerable impact on the success of a session.

The questions of how we are going to run the meeting, in what kind of room, and with what kind of evaluation are treated as the "smaller" questions. They become a later consideration, literally an afterthought.

I want to reverse what we call the "larger" and the "smaller" questions. The seemingly detailed concerns of how we engage the audience, in what kind of room, evaluated by what kind of questions, may have more to do with transforming a culture than the best strategy, structure, or clear, compelling presentation.[1]

No matter how skilled the facilitator, it is easy to overlook the enormous impact of these seemingly "smaller" administrative decisions. Overlooking these concerns can sabotage workshop outcomes, e.g., an inappropriate room size or number of participants can undermine the tone of a session and the quality of the discussion; choosing to make a workshop invitational instead of open to all interested parties can influence what people want to discuss or learn.

When workshops work well, these strategic management decisions are respected as important contributors to workshop outcomes. Problems are prevented and outcomes maximized, often without participants becoming aware of the time and energy required to make this happen. They simply notice that they feel good about the process: everything seems to run smoothly and better than anticipated. It is thoughtful consideration and deliberately creative decision making that makes this happen.

---

1. Block, Peter. *The Flawless Consulting Fieldbook and Companion.* San Francisco: Jossey-Bass/Pfeiffer, 2001, p. 150.

Method and Magic

At the heart of this systematic approach to workshop management are two key elements: method and magic.

Method involves two steps:

A. A thoughtful diagnosis of the workshop requirements based on eight categories (described in Chapter 2):

   1. Why this Workshop
   2. Workshop Coordinates
   3. Type of Session
   4. Roles, Responsibilities and Accountability
   5. Participants
   6. Context
   7. Pre-Session Package
   8. Best Scenario.

B. Careful decision making that complements the results of the Diagnostic Framework and surpasses expected outcomes.

Magic happens as a result of good method. Workshops with magic meet and exceed participants' and clients' expectations by enabling distinctive insights, surprising results or memorable experiences. As novelist Tom Robbins said: "Logic only gives man what he needs: magic gives him what he wants."

METHOD TO MAGIC

Diagnostic: You are organizing a community-based planning session to encourage consumer involvement in the developmental disabilities sector. One objective is to build confidence in consumer advocates and family members who are participating in the workshop.

Decisions: Create a glossary for participants that lists key words, phrases and acronyms in the developmental disabilities field. Send the glossary out in the pre-workshop package. Invite participants to suggest new acronyms and words.

This is the first time I've had my own mini-dictionary and it really helped me feel comfortable. As a new consumer representative, I'm not always in-the-know as much as others, so I liked the idea that I didn't have to ask others in the workshop about what a word or an acronym meant – this way I avoided slowing things down.

Getting From Method To Magic

While writing this handbook we talked a lot about workshop experiences that we have enjoyed. Without exception, these were well-managed workshops where:

- the right people were in the room to generate interesting, thoughtful ideas

- the agenda was clearly focused on fulfilling the purpose and objectives

- keynote speakers were on topic, within time limits and well oriented to expected outcomes

- time for discussion was protected

- food was served on time and it was fresh, interesting, at the right temperature and appropriate to the group

- participants' experiences in the topic area were valued and shared

- the session provided good value for the money

- participants were enthusiastic about the session and committed to acting on outcomes.

In these workshops, the organizers were in tune with participants' perspectives. They paid attention to the workshop as a whole system, managing both the tangible and intangible aspects of the system. They respected participants' time, experience and energy when considering how to have a productive and enjoyable session. They also made a special effort to anticipate their needs so that they felt comfortable in the workshop environment. The magic that resulted from these methods made these sessions memorable: something significantly positive happened for those present.

Anti-Magic Workshop Management

Most people have been to workshops or meetings that didn't work because the facilitator's personal style focused on her own strengths and areas of comfort at the expense of participants' interests. In these situations, a systematic diagnosis is lacking and decisions are made as a result of personal style rather than through reflection on workshop requirements. This rarely results in magic for participants.

Each of us has the potential to shift towards an anti-magic style when we focus more on our point of view than on the needs and perspectives of participants or clients. If we can recognize our potential for undermining magic, it is more likely that we will be able to prevent this from happening.

Following are six anti-magic workshop scenarios and some diagnostic questions to help prevent them in your sessions.

High Tech Teddy ensures that his team development sessions incorporate the latest in technology. Each participant has her own computer, and communication happens through shared electronic networks. There are very few discussions at a personal level: breaks and meals are used to catch up on email and what is going on at the office; discussions and decision making are through technology and voter keypads.

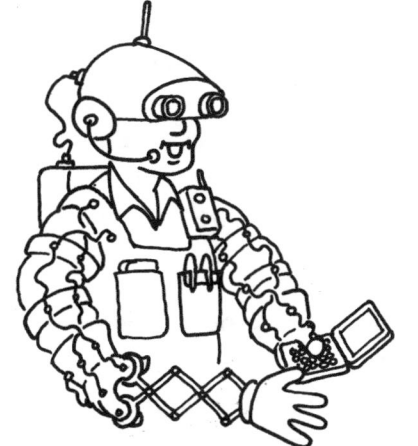

Teddy's management style: Teddy is more comfortable with technology and data than with people and ambiguity.

Diagnostic questions for Teddy: What are the appropriate types and amount of technology given this team-development workshop's purpose, expected outcomes and agenda? What is the most cost-effective technology? How could the technology support interpersonal communications?

Controlling Caroline is organizing her department's in-house strategic planning session. She has been doing this forever and is clear about how things should happen. She will do it the way she has always done it. She believes that planning committees are a waste of time because she has organized and evaluated previous sessions and is clear about how to make this a successful event. Seats are assigned and products pre-determined; objectives are not negotiable; nothing is left to chance. She often cuts people off during conversations.

Caroline's management style: Caroline feels most comfortable when she is completely in control.

Diagnostic questions for Caroline: Would a small, in-house organizing committee help build ownership for the outcomes of the planning session and for implementation at the operational level? Would the committee consider using an external facilitator to gather pre-meeting information, do a pre-session environmental scan, and enable Caroline to be a full participant during discussions? What can Caroline control that would ensure magic for participants?

Loosie Goosey Lucy is a spontaneous, fun-loving workshop facilitator who is not all that interested in session administration. Verbal contracts are fine with her – she believes in trust and really dislikes details. Her preference is for on-the-spot problem solving and informal management.

Sometimes workshop participants are not sure about the location of the hotel or about starting and finishing times but this is not a problem for Lucy. After all, these kinds of challenges just get people more involved in the process. Structured agendas are not her style – she likes to have a general purpose and just go with the flow – breaks and lunch will happen whenever. Reports are really superfluous. Sometimes, in moments of doubt or reflection, Lucy frets that she might be afraid to get better organized because it will raise everyone's expectations.

Lucy's management style: Objectives and outcomes are OK for some people but the looser things are, the more likely participants' needs and interests will emerge during a session. Planning and clarity make Lucy anxious about her ability to meet participants' needs.

Diagnostic questions for Lucy: Lucy has considerable interpersonal skills in enabling people to feel comfortable in difficult workshop situations. How can she maximize these skills without reducing her impact through administrative screw-ups? Is there someone in Lucy's department who could ensure that the managerial aspects of Lucy's sessions are well handled and outlined in a step-by-step plan?

Over Consulting Oliver is facilitating a one-day session on team building for 15 employees in the engineering section of his company. He has asked a human resources assistant in the personnel department to handle the workshop administration, including the development of the pre-session package. Oliver has instructed the assistant to: (a) send questionnaires to 250 internal customers to complete; (b) set up 55 interviews with external customers; and (c) write comprehensive reports on these inquiries. Reports on these consultations will be sent to each participant prior to the session. Each section employee who will be attending the session is also completing a questionnaire on preferences related to the workshop agenda and is filling out three individual assessment inventories related to leadership skills, team functioning and interpersonal skills.

Oliver's management style: Oliver figures he can never be prepared enough and session participants soon discover this. He doesn't believe that good decision making can happen unless there is a vast resource of background information to support discussion. Oliver is more comfortable with cognitive than intuitive approaches.

Diagnostic questions for Oliver: Given the team-building agenda for this session, what are the appropriate types and amount of pre-session information to support exploration of team issues? What are the strengths and weaknesses of this team and how can the pre-meeting package support team members in clarifying how they function as a team? Will this background information lure team members into intellectual discussions about test results when they should be focusing more on interpersonal dynamics and goals? How can team members develop more respect for their individual experience and intuitive capabilities in decision making rather than lean on large background information packages?

Anxious-to-Please Annie works in the conference administration section of a government department. She will do whatever her clients want without considering or voicing disagreement. Annie doesn't have clear boundaries on how much administration is appropriate for different types of workshops. She will provide as many reports as her client wants, although later she usually feels resentful.

Annie's management style: Annie feels best when she pleases her clients and they like her.

Diagnostic questions for Annie: What boundaries on her time does she need to ensure that others respect her expertise, time and resources? How can she implement standard review processes for reports so that others respect her time limitations? What steps can she take in her relationships with others to reduce the anxiety she feels when she's overly worried about pleasing people?

Bureaucratic Bill is organizing a one-day session on research priorities for 12 managers/supervisors in a 60 person mining company. The contract for the external facilitator is ten pages long. A steering committee of four researchers has developed a five-page critical path for three, two-hour meetings. The committee's Terms of Reference indicate that members will contribute their suggestions about the agenda and speakers.

Bill's management style: Bill is more comfortable with rules and procedures, paper and background material as indicators of success than with individual expertise and collaborative decision making. A sense of humour is not one of Bill's strengths – he takes his work very seriously.

Diagnostic questions for Bill: What is the most efficient and cost effective structure to support this meeting given that participants will also be taking part in several other planning and priority setting processes throughout the fiscal year? What is the appropriate amount of background information given the experience of participants and the sections in the agenda leading up to priority setting? Should the pre-meeting package be interactive and require participants to come prepared with a short list of priorities?

Each of these six caricatures has turned a strength into a liability, reducing the likelihood of outstanding experiences for participants. Keep an eye out for these anti-magic tendencies in yourself. Consider asking a colleague, co-facilitator or trusted person, "If I had a tendency to manifest one or more of these styles during a workshop, which one(s) would they be?"

Magic is about doing whatever will optimize a workshop experience for participants and clients. It is about going the extra mile to anticipate and respond to opportunities for delighting those involved. The more you act on this service commitment,[2] the more you develop and refine your intuition in relation to workshop management – that ability to sense what might benefit others.

> *We work on ourselves, then, in order to help others. And we help others as a vehicle for working on ourselves.*[3]

---

2. For further reading on "engaged service" see "Educating For a Deeper Sense of Self: Understanding, Compassion, and Engaged Service" in John P. Miller and Yoshiharu Nakagawa (eds.) *Nurturing our Wholeness: Perspectives on Spirituality in Education.* Brandon, Vermont: Foundation for Educational Renewal, 2002, p 309.
3. Ram Dass, Baba and Paul Gorman. *How Can I Help: Stories and Reflections on Service.* New York: Knopf. 1985, p. 227.

Chapter 2

A Diagnostic Framework

★★★★★★★★★★★★★★★★★★★★★★★

★★★★★★★★★★★★★★★★★★★★★★★

A Diagnostic Framework

A Diagnostic Framework organizes workshop requirements and takes the guesswork out of administrative decision making. Completing a diagnostic framework:

- **clarifies** the needs, hopes and concerns of clients and participants
- **supports** the development of a common vision for the workshop and its outcomes
- **raises questions** that focus your attention on key challenges and opportunities
- **educates** the client and/or workshop planning committee members about the potential effects of key administrative decisions on the success of the workshop, e.g., where a workshop is held, who is invited, how speakers are selected and briefed, the configuration of the room, content and format of the pre-session package, how the report is written
- **helps facilitators to clarify parameters,** organize a planning committee and prevent duplication of effort
- **generates a checklist** to ensure that the facilitation and management of the workshop are mutually supportive
- **supports collaborative decision making** by providing common reference points
- **gives you a starting point** for exploring, selecting and customizing tips, tools and templates (see Part II of this book) to fit the specifications and challenges identified through the framework.

" The first time I used this diagnostic framework to get ready for a workshop, I felt a little overwhelmed. But as I worked my way through the first couple of categories, I found that it organized my thinking and pointed out areas that I had forgotten. "

In summary, using a diagnostic framework enables you to clarify and confirm how and why things should happen in service of the workshop purpose and objectives. Raising these questions sooner rather than later in the planning process enables you to prevent potential problems from arising during a session.

However, workshop management also requires flexibility as specifications can change midstream: you may have been given a participant quota of 30, only to have it expanded to 50; a decision to hold a session in a downtown setting may be switched to a rural retreat.

If you are working from a diagnostic framework when these changes happen, you have the information at your fingertips to help you make adjustments that will continue to support expected outcomes.

> *" I took a big step forward as a facilitator when I realized that being well prepared does not mean being inflexible. "*

At first blush, completing a diagnostic framework with eight categories and various sub-sections may seem overly time-consuming and complicated. Taking the time to complete this framework up front is a solid investment in preventing problems and promoting success. It's a comprehensive workshop management planning process in five pages.

Eight Categories

This workshop diagnostic framework has eight categories related to workshop management:

1. Why this Workshop
2. Workshop Coordinates
3. Type of Session
4. Roles, Responsibilities and Accountability
5. Participants
6. Context
7. Pre-Session Package
8. Best Scenario.

A template for this framework is included at the end of this chapter.

Although each category in the framework is a separate entity, all eight categories are interdependent when it comes to making decisions. For example, if the name of an invitational planning workshop (category #2) isn't compelling, it may be difficult to get the kind of participants (category #5) needed to ensure quality decision making. Or if the right background information (category #7) isn't available, it may be hard to make decisions during the session. By completing the categories in the framework early in the planning process, you raise these challenges for consideration sooner rather than later.

The following outlines describe the information required for each category.

1. Why this Workshop

The more clarity there is about the purpose and objectives of a session, the more you can target your methods to support expected outcomes. Once you have written the purpose and objectives, ask yourself:

- Given these objectives, what implications do you see for managing the session?

  " Last year's workshop for our car plant was on North American trade issues. The workshop organizers set the sessions up in both Windsor and Detroit so we could get a deeper understanding of both cultures. "

- Sessions usually have process objectives such as networking and team building in addition to the development of products such as a strategic plan. What are the process objectives for this session? What are the implications of these objectives (if any) for you as a workshop manager?

> *" I felt clear about where we were going and how we were going to get there throughout this whole workshop. The facilitator posted the objectives at the front of the room and then ticked them off as we went through them. We even checked in a couple of times on how we felt we were doing as members of the team. Our focus was always right under our noses. "*

2. Workshop Coordinates

Ask yourself the following questions when considering a workshop name, date and location.

Name

- Is it short and to the point?
- Does it describe what the session is about?
- What makes it attractive to potential workshop participants, the client, sponsors, key stakeholders?
- Are the workshop outcomes reflected in the name?

Date

- Does the date provide enough preparation time for participants and planners?
- What would make this date attractive to potential workshop participants?
- Are other events going on at this time (or near) that may complement or conflict with this session? Should this session happen in a sequence with other sessions?
- How close is the date to national, provincial or state, religious or school holidays?

Location

- What setting would work best for our purposes, e.g., ambience, accessibility and size of workshop rooms?
- Is there someone you can talk to who has experience with this location?
- Is adequate parking available?
- What might make this location attractive or unattractive to potential workshop participants? What will participants be able to do during off hours at this location?

Sometimes participants at the same session will have radically different perspectives related to workshop coordinates.

> " *I really liked being isolated in a country inn, especially when things are such a zoo at work. It forced us to gel as a team – there wasn't anything else to do.* "
>
> OR
>
> " *Why did you do this out in no man's land? There was nothing to do and nowhere to go. Next time, book this session somewhere in town where we can shop, go to a movie, find a cozy restaurant.* "

3. Type of Session

Some workshops are formal, institutionalized events such as orientation sessions for new employees, strategic planning retreats or team development sessions; others are informal learning situations involving six to nine people meeting in a community hall; still others are educational sessions within a larger conference or an annual general meeting.

Different workshops require different methods. A consultation at an Annual General Meeting often involves large numbers of decision makers speaking from their organizations' perspectives. A strategic planning workshop for account managers in a regional office may involve a small number of key supervisors who want to align their operations with the corporation's strategic goals. By clarifying and naming the type of session requiring facilitation and administration you move beyond the generic label of "workshop" and begin to set expectations and parameters related to administrative requirements.

Following is a chart outlining 15 types of sessions that require customized "methods" to get to "magic." Once you identify what type of workshop is involved, many decisions about method become clearer. The chart provides examples of implications for decisions about workshop management; it is not intended to address all decisions.

Some sessions can be described by more than one type. For example, you may be organizing a "consultation workshop" or a "roundtable seminar." Similarly, some organizations develop their own names for sessions that are combinations of these types: an extended residential seminar workshop that moves across the country may be called a study tour; a regularly scheduled seminar roundtable may be called a network.

> " *Using a think tank format took a lot of pressure off us. We knew we were just giving it our best shot in terms of advice, and that we didn't have to make decisions that involved accountability. This helped us to just let go and be creative.* "

Different types of workshops raise different considerations for decisions about method. By clarifying up front what type of workshop you are facilitating/managing, you can explore implications for administrative decisions early in the planning cycle.

Part I: Workshop Management That Works

Type of Session	Description	Participation	Presentations	Decision Making	Room Set-up
Annual General Meeting	Regular session (e.g., annually) with board members and membership of not-for-profit groups and other organizations; focus is primarily on reporting on the past year and making key decisions for the future	For members, by invitation	On business items; AV usually required; copies of presentations often provided in background documents	Usually; may require electronic voting if large numbers	Often large numbers; may need rooms for small groups; often recorded; microphones on tables
Chartered Forum	Regular meetings of an organization's board of directors focused on the policies and related decisions required to manage the business as described in the organization's strategic plan	For members, by invitation; may also include guests and new members	On new approaches and issues; presentation outlines provided	Sometimes	Virtual and real time discussions in small groups and plenary
Colloquium	An academic conference or seminar focused on dialogue and conversation	Open to all who are interested	On related topics; provide copies of presentations	Rarely	To enable discussions in plenary and informal small groups
Conference	A large (usually) gathering that brings together people who want to hear about, learn or discuss important matters in a specific area	May be open to all interested parties or invitational to members or specific groups	On a variety of topics; AV required	Sometimes	Varies according to the agenda and the numbers involved

A Diagnostic Framework

Type of Session	Description	Participation	Presentations	Decision Making	Room Set-up
Consultation	A workshop or longer process (e.g., a series of workshops or focus groups) where participants speak from their positions – often as representatives of groups or organizations – and are encouraged to advocate their points of view; participants have the right to advise but not to decide; they may consult with one another or be consulted by another party or both	May be invitational or open to interested individuals and groups	Sometimes, usually to describe the current situation	No	Eye contact among participants; tables for taking notes
Forum	A formal meeting for public discussion	Open to interested parties	Usually at the start followed by Q and A	No	Varies; often theatre style due to formality
Kick-off Meeting	An initial session of a longer project or process where the focus is on building enthusiasm for and generating basic understanding of an agenda, key themes or issues	Invitational to a specific group	Yes, usually with handouts	No	May be informal with participants standing or more formal with tables and chairs
Roundtable[4]	A workshop where participants share equal influence and status; most roundtables process information on a subject with a view towards decision making by others after the roundtable	Invitational	No, except for opening remarks	Depends on purpose	Seating arrangement reflects equality of participants, e.g., circle or hexagon, no head table, unless used by facilitator
Search Conference	An opportunity to discover common ground and imagine an ideal future through methods of discovery, analysis and dialogue that broaden perspectives, expand horizons and lead to committed action[5]	Invitational or open to interested parties	Yes, usually to focus discussions that follow	Sometimes, e.g., in action planning	Varies in response to the agenda; may use open space approach

4. The term "Roundtable" comes from the roundtable at which King Arthur and his chosen knights sat so that none would have precedence.
5. Weisbord, Marvin R. et al, *Discovering Common Ground*. San Francisco, CA: Berrett Koehler Publishers, 1992, p. xiii.

Type of Session	Description	Participation	Presentations	Decision Making	Room Set-up
Seminar	An intensive course of study on a specific topic; often a meeting of specialists; usually small in size; may be set up as a study tour, e.g., a week-long travelling tour focused on a specific topic	By invitation to a specific profession or group of interested people	Yes, focused on a specific topic area; provide copies/outlines	No	Varies; often theatre style with formal Q&A following presentations
Summit	A conference where leading people in an area meet to discuss and come to agreement on key considerations for the future of an area	By invitation to current or future leaders in a field	Usually	Usually recommendations to others, rather than decisions	Speakers' table at front, podium, small round tables for participants or open space
Symposium	An opportunity to learn from experts and discuss ideas with colleagues	By invitation to a specific profession or group of interested people	Yes	No	Varies; often theatre style with formal Q and A following presentations
Town Hall Meeting	An open, informal gathering where general presentations are made and preliminary views on a subject are explored	Open Invitation	Yes	No	Varies; often informal; space for moving around
Think Tank	A group or body of experts, key informants or opinion leaders providing advice and ideas on a specific topic, issue or challenge	Invitational to people with experience or expertise	Yes, often to encourage creativity and innovation	Results in recommendations to others rather than decisions	Eye contact among participants; tables for taking notes; space for moving around
Workshop	A facilitated process that happens in a limited time period, e.g., a few hours, a day, a weekend, a week. Regardless of format, objectives, orientation or size, workshops actively involve individuals and groups in doing "work" that is focused on specific outcomes	Open or invitational	Depends on objectives	Depends on objectives	Eye contact among participants; tables for taking notes; may not need breakout rooms for small groups

4. Roles, Responsibilities and Accountability

The workshop facilitator is ultimately accountable for ensuring that the management of a session supports the purpose, objectives and expected outcomes. However, the devil in this plan is certainly in the details as there are often several other people involved in making a workshop a success, e.g., a planning committee, an organization's support staff, hotel employees, travel agents, an audiovisual company, conference and maintenance personnel at the session site.

The six sections in this part of the framework help ensure that everyone involved in developing the workshop is clear about the planning structure, roles, responsibilities, accountabilities and who is communicating with whom.

- a. Client
- b. Contact Person
- c. Planning Structure
- d. Facilitation
- e. Management
- f. Key Deliverables

Sometimes a minor communication error can turn magic to muddle, thwarting your efforts to build a memorable experience for participants. Be absolutely clear about who the client is, e.g., is it your main liaison person or her boss? Or is it an outside funder?

Keep your diagnostic framework handy so that you can refer to it during meetings when people ask who is doing what by when. The framework is a multi-use tool that serves as a guideline for keeping roles and relationships on track. It can be revised as people and positions change throughout the workshop preparation period.

> *" Over a four month period prior to a workshop we (steering committee members) consulted our framework several times to clarify roles and responsibilities. We were all scattered around the country and were working together by teleconference. Sometimes the decisions we made over the phone just didn't have the same clarity and impact of those made during our face-to-face meetings. People couldn't remember exactly what we had discussed or agreed to and they started to duplicate what others were doing. Being able to refer to a framework really helped us iron out these wrinkles. "*

5. Participants

    a. Who

    b. Invitations

    c. Participation

The purpose and objectives of a session usually dictate the type, number and involvement of participants.

- Training sessions that are open to the public and focus on interpersonal skill development usually work better with smaller numbers of participants who will have lots of opportunity to interact with others and practise new skills.

- If you work for a professional association and are organizing a roundtable for experts on personalized banking, invitations will probably be sent to individuals with expertise in various aspects of the topic. Participants are likely to be busy, so your invitation will need to entice them to come to the session (see Chapter 5). Several factors related to how the session is being managed will influence their decision to attend, e.g., who else is coming, guest speakers, potential benefits, location, amenities.

The nature and number of participants also have an impact on a wide variety of management decisions. For example:

- If you are conducting a large consultation with scientific experts in a controversial ethical area, you may need to arrange for an electronic voting system to encourage inclusiveness and record opinions anonymously.

- If you are organizing a board development session for a not-for-profit organization with a history of significant conflict among board members, ensure that the room set-up encourages direct eye contact and lots of opportunity for small buzz groups, e.g., a hexagon with two or three people per side for plenary sessions and quick consultations.

> *This session was great. You had the right people here and the group was just the right size. I thought this had a positive impact on the quality of our discussions so I'm feeling really good about our decisions. And for the first time in three years I'm looking forward to making all this stuff happen.*

For further considerations related to participants, see Chapter 4.

6. Context

Context addresses the workshop surroundings and how they weave together to give a picture of the current situation, e.g., organizational working conditions; connections to related departments and other organizations; historical, social and cultural implications of the workshop; what is going on in related areas before, during and after the workshop; issues on the public agenda that relate to the workshop objectives.

> *A few years ago I facilitated/managed a policy development process for a public sector client in aircraft safety. We had completed the final workshop report before we discovered that another branch of government was in the process of developing a related policy and that we should have been working together to avoid duplication.*

Whether you are working internally or externally, chances are that you will need to gather background information that enables you to understand fully the unique management challenges presented by a workshop.

Suppose you are an external facilitator who has been asked to conduct account planning sessions for sales personnel in a high-tech company. You discover that the work environment is hectic, extremely competitive, and that account managers are expected to be available to both their managers and clients on an on-going basis. During discussions with the regional manager you identify managers'/participants' time pressures and accountabilities and together you make the following decisions in support of their full participation at the workshop:

- participation in the session is mandatory for all account managers
- phones, pagers and email are off during the retreat
- breaks are for 30 minutes every 1.5 hours to enable participants to access voicemail updates and return urgent calls
- the workshop site has excellent cell phone reception
- a senior vice-president opens the retreat and makes clear links between the purpose of the planning session and the overall corporate goals for the next two years.

As a result of these decisions related to context, participants are comfortable focusing on the topics at hand: they know that you are looking out for their best interests both in the workshop and outside it and that they will have an opportunity to return calls and complete customer service cycles at opportune times throughout the retreat. Account managers who were inclined to resist strategic planning have fewer concerns because everyone on the team is present for the entire agenda; the session is supported by senior management; and they feel their time is valued and appreciated. This is method to magic: you have taken participants' perspectives on what would make this workshop a success and then acted on their needs and interests.

7. Pre-Session Package

Getting the right type and amount of background information to support your role as workshop facilitator/manager can be tricky. Too much information can be as problematic as not enough information, or the wrong type of information.

The best pre-workshop packages help to create a level playing field for participants: they ensure that everyone involved in the session has access to the same baseline information. The questions in this section of the framework explore what existing or new documentation is required so that people can participate comfortably and with confidence.

8. Best Scenario

   a. Expectations

   b. Concerns

   c. Management Challenges

Most people involved in planning a workshop have an image of what a really great workshop would look and feel like. If you ask members of your organizing committee to describe this "best scenario," you can discuss similarities and differences in perspectives, clarify expectations and ensure that everyone is working towards the same outcomes. This clarification process puts concerns on the table and helps to identify workshop management challenges, thus easing tensions and generating energy for making the workshop function well.

> *" Checking assumptions about a best scenario could have saved me a lot of grief with this particular client. I initially assumed that a board development session for an international not-for-profit organization involving 12 new board members out of a total of 27 would work best in a fairly informal setting where people had an opportunity to meet each other, share experiences and discuss roles and responsibilities. "*

> *"The new president of the board had a completely different perspective. He wanted a formal reception with a prestigious speaker, followed by a lecture by him on effective boardroom behaviour. He didn't want board members to interact much as he felt this would encourage the development of political alliances in a situation already fraught with tension and disagreement.*
>
> *As the facilitator, I encouraged him to take a less formal and more open approach. However, he wanted a controlled environment where he could make his expectations clear about power and politics for the future. It was his call. If I had had an opportunity to discuss best scenarios with him earlier, I might have reconsidered getting involved."*

You can clarify best scenarios by asking the questions listed in the diagnostic framework on page 31.

Completing a Diagnostic Framework

The purpose of this framework is to support strategic decision making, not to encourage a standardized way of doing workshops. In fact, when the diagnostic framework works well, its efficiency enables you to free up time and energy for thinking more creatively about ways to customize the session in the interests of participants.

Each workshop is a unique entity with its own particular specifications and set of circumstances. Some sections of the framework are obvious and can be completed quickly. Other sections may take some discussion and consideration to finalize with your client or planning committee. More information related to the categories in the framework is provided in Part II of this book.

There are several ways to complete a diagnostic framework. We find it works best when we use it as a vehicle to enable discussion or to set an agenda for a meeting. For example:

- Fill it out by yourself and then share specific sections with your client, customer or workshop planning committee to check your assumptions. This provides stakeholders with an opportunity to clarify the key decisions that will have an impact on the purpose and outcomes of the session.

- Bring the framework to your first meeting with a client to help set an agenda for a teleconference with the session planning committee. Have extra copies on hand in case you want to distribute them.

- Use it yourself as a way to stay on track; don't share it with your client. For some clients, a diagnostic framework is TMI - too much information.

- Use the outline to confirm that your contract is covering all the bases. Sometimes, as a result of completing the framework, we will discover that there is more effort involved on our part than had originally seemed to be the case.

> *" I use the framework as a forget-me-not tool – it gets completed in different ways for different kinds of sessions. The first thing I usually do is go through the entire thing and fill in whatever I already know. Then I highlight areas that I think I should discuss with my client at the first meeting and then during later discussions. In other situations, where I have a lot of experience with a particular client, I can fill most of it in myself. "*

TEMPLATE 2.1
WORKSHOP DIAGNOSTIC FRAMEWORK

1. Why this Workshop

The purpose of this workshop is to:
_____
_____

The client's most important outcome is:
_____

Review the workshop purpose and check the following relevant objectives that apply, customizing them as required. Then rank them from most to least important.

__ analyze issues, approaches

__ brainstorm new ideas and explore innovative approaches

__ clarify values

__ conduct a consultation

__ create a vision

__ develop a plan, e.g., operational, strategic, account

__ develop policies

__ develop recommendations for action

__ do some problem solving

__ enable education, learning and skill development

__ enable networking

__ enhance group functioning

__ explore ethics

__ generate a list of key questions

__ make decisions

__ motivate improved performance

__ share information

__ support behaviour change

Other: _____ Other: _____

2. Workshop Coordinates

Name of the session: _____

Date: _____

Location: _____

Part I: Workshop Management That Works

3. Type of Session

__ Annual General Meeting
__ Chartered Forum
__ Colloquium
__ Conference
__ Consultation
__ Forum
__ Kick-off Meeting
__ Roundtable

__ Search Conference
__ Seminar
__ Summit
__ Symposium
__ Town Hall Meeting
__ Think Tank
__ Workshop
__ Other/Combination: _____

4. Roles, Responsibilities and Accountability

Client (for accountability)		Phone: Email:
Contact Person (for liaison)		Phone: Email:

Planning Structure

__ Client

__ Volunteer staff planning committee

__ Designated staff planning committee

__ Volunteer planning committee

__ Volunteer planning committee with a small core working group

__ Program committee with input to the agenda

__ Steering committee providing oversight to the committee

__ Expert advisory panel providing input on the agenda

__ Geographical teams, e.g., by province, state, region or municipality

__ Divisional teams, e.g., by corporate sector

__ External meeting planner

Other: _____

Facilitation

Type	Who
Chair	
Co-chairs: volunteer chairs working together	
Co-chairs: volunteer chair and professional facilitator working together	
External volunteer or professional facilitator	
Internal volunteer or professional facilitator	
Table facilitators	
Other:	

Management

Type	Who
By the facilitator	
Volunteer(s)	
Contractor	
Secretariat, e.g., government, not-for-profit	
Committee	

Key Deliverables

Description, e.g., questionnaire, reports	When	Who
1.		
2.		
3.		
4.		
5.		

5. Participants

Total # Expected	# of Local Participants	# Requiring Travel and Accommodation

Invitations

__ By invitation only

__ Limited by categories, e.g., 25% professionals, 25% advocates

__ Mandatory

__ Open to all

__ Invited by categories, e.g., age, gender, profession, qualifications, interest areas, geographical location

__ Restricted to membership

__ Restricted to specific groups and organizations

__ Voluntary by categories, e.g., sales managers and accountants

Other: _____

During the workshop, participants:

__ Have equal status in discussion and decision making

__ Maintain positional influence and authority in the organization during the workshop

__ Represent organizations

__ Represent different perspectives

__ Participate without prejudice, i.e., they share information or provide input without commitment to outcomes

__ Participate without prejudice but with a commitment to possible action depending on outcomes, i.e., they provide input and commit to (a) sharing the workshop outcomes with their groups or organizations and (b) asking how the organization might like to be involved in the future

__ Collaborate on planning the workshop, e.g., providing input on purpose, agenda, outcomes, reports, implementation, through prior consultations

__ Are resource persons or are in participant-observer roles; they do not influence discussion or decision making

Other: _____

6. Context

Who initiated this workshop?

What motivated the development of this workshop?

What is the justification for the time and expense required to do this workshop?

Who will use the workshop results and for what purpose?

What amenities will participants need to feel comfortable being away from their workplaces or homes for this period of time?

What are the biggest stressors these participants are likely to experience in their day-to-day lives? Which of these stressors could we ameliorate during this session?

Are there any accepted ground rules for meetings that they would like to follow during this workshop?

Who else might be interested in what happens at this session?

How will the results of the workshop be shared?

6. Context (cont'd)

What related initiatives and documents (meetings, reports, surveys, polls, organizational processes, plans, etc.) are going on or planned for the near future?

Initiative: _____

Purpose and Objectives: _____

Links to this workshop: _____

7. Pre-Session Package

What existing or new information/documentation needs to be included to enable attendees to participate fully and with confidence? Consider supportive pieces such as lists of key terms, acronyms, web sites, organizations and networks, as well as relevant publications and bibliographies suggested in Section #6: Context.

8. Best Scenario

Imagine that this workshop has been over for a week and you are delighted with how everything turned out. What happened that made this session so successful from your perspective?

If this is what you would like to see happen at this workshop, what are the main management challenges that need to be addressed? For each challenge, discuss options for action.

Challenge: _____

Options for Action: _____

Challenge: _____

Options for Action: _____

Chapter 3

Decision Making

★ ★

★ ★

Decision Making

Chapter 2 provided a diagnostic framework for clarifying the needs, hopes and concerns of clients and participants from their perspectives. This chapter describes two aspects of decision making related to implementing the results of the diagnostic framework:

A. Structure – Workshop decision-making structures include the people and systems you put in place to plan, organize and administer a session.

B. Process – The decision-making process has two parts: (a) choosing and customizing tools and templates, and (b) creating opportunities to add value.

The following example illustrates how structure and process work hand-in-hand for effective decision making.

METHOD TO MAGIC

Diagnostic: You are facilitating/managing a team-development workshop with 23 employees of a National Education Institute. Senior managers at the Institute are concerned about employee morale due to overwork and the negative public perception of the Institute.

Decisions: Create a workshop steering committee made up of three people representing employee groups at the workshop. Hold the workshop at a location that reflects the results of research in wellness education. Make decisions about meals, breaks and opportunities for physical activity based on the Institute's recent work on stress management. Provide a gift certificate for a free stress test as a door prize. (value-add). Order nutritious, light lunches so that participants don't feel lethargic during afternoon sessions. Provide recipe cards on tables (value-add). Ask for cell phones and pagers to be turned off during sessions to reduce stress and prevent distractions.

For the first time since I started work here seven years ago, I couldn't see any contradictions between how we were treated and what our research says about wellness education. Great location, good pacing, tasty food, great recipes, lots of opportunities for activity. Thanks to the steering committee, I left feeling good about my work.

A. Structure

Structures vary, depending on the size, purpose and outcomes of a session. For small, simple workshops, a structure might be two people: you as the facilitator/manager and your client. For larger, more complex workshops, you may want to have a structure that includes a four-person organizing committee that does most of the hands-on work, a program committee for input on the agenda and speakers, and a larger, representative steering committee that advises on key issues.

Size

Size matters. Keep the number of committee members involved as low as possible, while satisfying requirements outlined in the Diagnostic Framework (Chapter 2). The fewer the people, the easier it is to set up meetings, make decisions and communicate with one another.

For larger workshops, when more than one committee or group is involved in providing oversight, build continuity between groups by having one or two people on all committees, i.e., before, during and after the workshop. To provide continuity and a "reality check," ensure that you have one or two workshop participants as members of your main organizing group.

Composition: Getting the Right People

Think about the characteristics and skills required in your structure to support effective decision making. Do you need:

- Respected "big picture" strategic thinkers who focus on how the results of the workshop will affect current organizational challenges?

- Senior individuals inside an organization with the authority to make key decisions?

- Thoughtful, analytical outsiders who can provide advice on related external perspectives on issues?

- Well-connected people who can help to market the session, or who have media influence?

- People with the credibility required to help implement the workshop results?

- Individuals with high levels of content expertise?

- Grass roots political organizers with strong community connections?

- Administrators with strong organization and people management skills?

- People who can remain creative and cool when dealing with difficult people and unexpected crises?

> *" Our planning committee only had six people on it and yet we pretty much represented the key perspectives in our region. We were three men and three women with one rep from each Unit. Half were union, the other half management. There were some really experienced people as well as a couple of newer types who had some different ideas about how we could do things. On the whole it was pretty efficient and we always knew what was happening. "*

Terms of Reference

To support quality decision making, define a clear role for the organizing group through a Terms of Reference. Whether two or 20 people are involved, clarify purpose, assumptions, roles, responsibilities, how decisions will be made, communication processes and the structure that will support individuals as they work together to make things happen. The more clarity you bring to functions, the better the decision making and communication will be for all involved.

A committee Terms of Reference should include the following basic components.

Purpose	an overall statement describing the organizing group's mandate or functions
Assumptions and Guiding Principles	the basic tenets that support what you are doing and how you are doing it
Decision Making	how the group will make decisions, e.g., voting, consensus, by authority of the chair
Membership	criteria for committee members and number of members
Term of Appointment	start to finish date
Meetings	frequency, length, type, travel, leadership
Communication	how, who, confidentiality, disclosure to workshop participants, between meetings, media involvement
Reporting	how, to whom, frequency.

> *" It took us about six weeks and three teleconferences to develop a terms of reference for our national forum. Every minute we spent on it paid off in the end. Although it was frustrating at times, going through this process made sure we were all on the same wavelength. We clarified all the key issues up front with both the steering committee and the planning committee so they didn't pop up unexpectedly later. "*

Responsibilities

Following is a range of potential responsibilities to consider when determining the functions of a workshop organizing group. Give committee members some choice about the specific responsibilities and commitment they would like to assume. Some may want to be involved in very hands-on roles while others may have more advisory roles in mind. Their responses will have implications for workloads and responsibilities.

a. Review and agree on:
   - the workshop purpose, objectives and expected outcomes
   - resources required, where they will come from and who will be responsible for obtaining them.

b. Develop:
   - the key assumptions and guiding principles that underlie the purpose and objectives
   - criteria for who should participate (see Chapter 4)
   - a list of invitees
   - a workshop name.

c. Contribute ideas regarding:
   - the agenda
   - speakers
   - an invitation or announcement
   - how small groups might be constituted, e.g., on the basis of expertise or geography
   - opening and closing remarks
   - content of the background information package, e.g., fact sheets, research, reports
   - the views of groups, organizations, or jurisdictions that members are representing.

d. Support:
    - a positive communication process before, during and after the workshop
    - the workshop process by lending the credibility of their names, experience and expertise
    - implementation of workshop outcomes
    - continuity between sessions that are part of a series.

e. Participate in:
    - organizing committee meetings, committing to a specified time-frame, e.g., five meetings of two hours each
    - the workshop, taking on organizing roles as required, e.g., welcoming people, helping with registration, supporting the workshop ground rules, providing feedback to the facilitator and liaison with the hotel on logistics
    - representing the purpose and objectives of the session to people outside of the process such as those who may not be directly involved with the session but will be affected by decisions made during the session
    - liaising with groups or individuals identified by organizing committees, e.g., partner organizations, individuals, those who are unable to attend meetings.

f. Advise on:
    - big-picture aspects of the session, e.g., how things fit together conceptually, where linkages need to happen with other organizations, how to address implementation challenges
    - an on-going basis as required, e.g., testing ideas on workshop development, whether the agenda will satisfy the workshop goals and objectives, background documentation.

g. Review draft workshop reports and support their implementation.

> *" Building agreement on a terms of reference with an organizing committee puts decision-making power into the hands of a small group whose members reflect a range of perspectives and also have a vested interest in the session outcomes. This starts to build ownership for the workshop, which is a big help when it comes to implementing outcomes. From an organizer's perspective, they are writing the songbook that they're going to sing from throughout the entire workshop process. "*

What's in a Name?

Naming a structure such as an organizing committee is an important part of defining how people will be involved in making and implementing decisions about a workshop. People select names for several reasons: they may be tired of words like "committee" or "task force"; they may want to indicate the structure's authority, whether decision-making or advising; and/or they may want to signal a specific timeframe, an area of responsibility or a degree of formality. Following are some options to consider when naming committees and groups in your workshop management structure. Match the functions in the left column with a type in the right column, e.g., coordinating group, review panel, oversight committee.

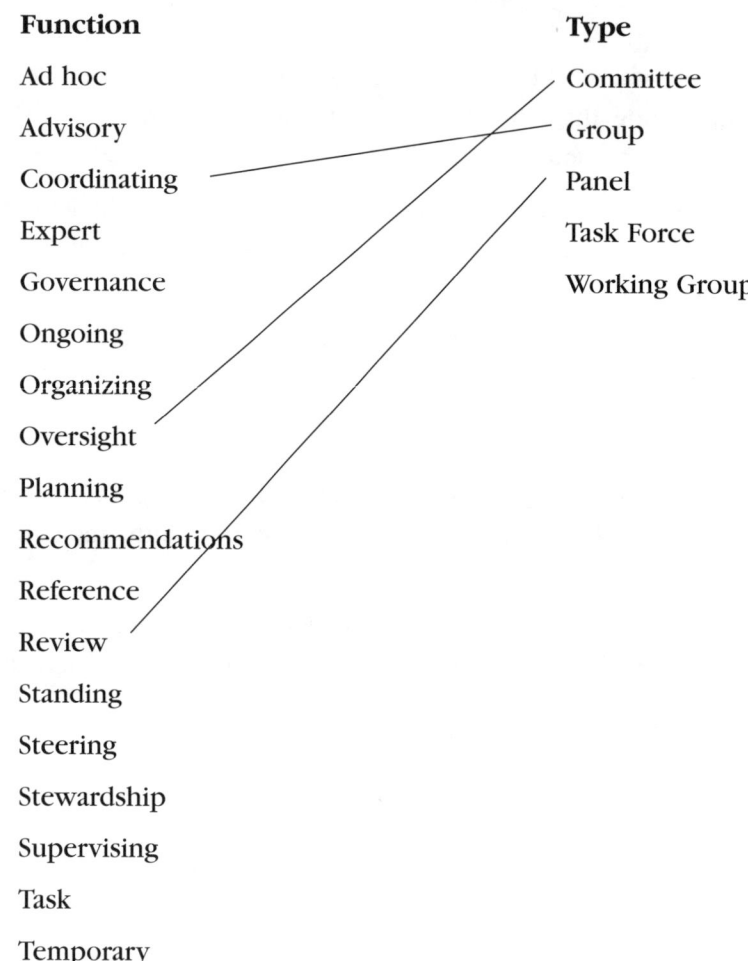

Function	Type
Ad hoc	Committee
Advisory	Group
Coordinating	Panel
Expert	Task Force
Governance	Working Group
Ongoing	
Organizing	
Oversight	
Planning	
Recommendations	
Reference	
Review	
Standing	
Steering	
Stewardship	
Supervising	
Task	
Temporary	

Managing Meetings

Meetings that work are efficient, enjoyable and provide participants with a sense of accomplishment.

> " *Being part of the organizing committee was an unexpected bonus. We were small and fast. And we made some great decisions. I learned a lot about how to put on one of these things and also how to run high-productivity meetings. It was a really impressive group of people – I'm going to collaborate with a couple of others on the committee to write the report and it's going into a professional journal. Not what I expected at all.* "

The workshop manager/facilitator has an influential role in making the organizing committee's meetings successful. Think about the sequence of activities before, during and after each meeting, as well as during the workshop.

Before meetings:

- Develop an easy-to-use workplan with timelines and dates and stick to it, updating and revising as the situation evolves.

- Remind individuals about the tasks they agreed to complete and report back on; discuss the time (number of minutes) they will require on the agenda; check if they have documents to be distributed or presentation requirements.

- Discuss the agenda with the chairperson in advance of the meeting. Ensure all items are appropriate for the meeting agenda, i.e., that they require discussion and a decision by the group, not just by an individual.

- Plan to arrive before the scheduled meeting time so that you can try out any required equipment or technology to ensure it is in working order, e.g., teleconference arrangements are functioning smoothly.

- Ensure the location is set up so that everyone can see and hear each other.

- For distance technology meetings, e.g., teleconferences:
    - Ensure meetings are conveniently timed for everyone. Clarify and confirm the different start times in members' respective time zones.
    - Ensure the meeting chair knows what to do if service problems arise or more time is required.
    - Be prepared for service peculiarities related to technology, e.g., provide a backup number in case something goes wrong.
    - The day before the meeting, check to ensure that everyone has received their documents.

- Sometimes facilitators/managers become involved with a workshop after a planning group or steering committee is already in place. In this situation, review the group's mandate and ask questions to clarify how you will work with this group:
    - What does this group make decisions about and how do they make them?
    - What meetings have been held to date regarding this workshop?
    - Are minutes available from previous meetings?
    - What key decisions have been made?
    - Has there been any previous correspondence distributed in relation to this session?
    - What action has been taken on previous meetings?
    - Has anyone else been involved in planning the workshop so far?
    - Are there any sources of tension or "hot spots" that you should be aware of?

During meetings:

- Provide an updated workplan so that people feel that they are making progress as the workshop gets closer.

- Prepare members for questions that they may be asked, e.g.,

    Q: *How did you get on the International Organizing Committee?*

    A: *I was nominated by my community based on criteria developed by the One Sky Initiative.*

After meetings:

- Reflect on how it went:
    - What did you like about your role in the meeting?
    - If you could do it over again, what would you do differently?

Working with Other Meeting Professionals

In some sessions your decision-making structure may include other meeting planners.[2] In these situations it is still your responsibility as the facilitator to ensure that the workshop is managed in support of the purpose and objectives of the process, not just for efficiency or cost effectiveness.

Be clear about what responsibilities belong to whom: Who determines the type of speakers required? Who will set up audiovisual equipment? Who does the liaison with speakers to ensure that they fit well into the agenda and respond to the needs of participants? If a professional meeting planner is more accustomed to working on large conferences and seminars, he may not be familiar with your role and responsibility as a facilitator in ensuring that the management of the session directly supports the group process.

> *" Recently, when working with professional meeting planners to prepare for a large conference on small business investment, there was some initial confusion about why we were involved as professional facilitators. The meeting planners were accustomed to asking their clients what type of speaker they should get, providing some suggestions and then following through with a contract. When we explained that the speaker needed to fit into a process based on adult learning principles and that the presentation should prepare people for some group work immediately afterward, the relationship between the facilitators and the meeting planners started to become clear.*
>
> *The decision was that we (as facilitators) would determine the type of speaker required (experience, competencies, presentation style) and then the client and meeting planners would generate a list of possibilities. The final decision would be made jointly. The responsibility of the meeting planners would be to explore costs, develop a contract and hire the speaker and we would work with the speaker to ensure that she would fit into the conference design. "*

Support a close and respectful relationship with other meeting professionals such as planners, translators and technologists so that you can work together comfortably, respecting each other's contributions toward making the workshop successful. Discuss the workshop tone (e.g., formal, informal) with your client and how decisions related to workshop management can support the development of that tone in service of expected outcomes.

---

2. Meeting Planners International. Note that the roles of meeting manager and meeting coordinator are distinct in this organization.

    MPI International Headquarters: 4455 LBJ Freeway, Suite 1200, Dallas, Texas, Voice: +1-972-702-3000 U.S.A. 75244-5903, Fax: +1-972-702-3070. www.mpiweb.org.

Make positive politics[3] a guiding principle during planning processes. Positive politics involve all of the activities that people engage in to gain support for their ideas. This may include persuasive discussions and marshalling support for a particular perspective. Political processes are a normal and predictable part of workshop management and if carried on in a positive manner, can contribute significantly to the vitality of an organizing committee by providing an opportunity for people to clarify their ideas, engage in constructive discussion and help to determine the path they want the workshop to take. Committee or task force meetings provide an opportunity to model how the workshop itself will be managed in terms of positive politics.

3. Strachan, Dorothy et al. *Volunteers Working Together*. Ottawa: Government of Canada, Fitness and Amateur Sport, Skills Program for Management Volunteers, 1986: p 97 - 100. Adapted. See also Block, Peter. *The Empowered Manager. Positive Political Skills at Work*. San Francisco: Jossey-Bass, 1987.

B. Process

In workshop management, the best decisions generate the most magic. The following two-part decision-making process can significantly leverage outcomes for participants and clients.

- Choose and customize the tools and templates in Part II that complement the results of your diagnostic framework.

- Create additional opportunities to add value. A "value-add" is a positive and unexpected impact that contributes to an exceptional workshop experience. Value-adds are not included in contracts: they are over and above client and participant expectations.

Although this process can be described in two parts, in reality, decision making is not quite so neat. Most decisions evolve from a combination of experience, imagination and communication with others involved in organizing a workshop.[4] The experience part is based on what people have learned from similar past situations; the imagination sparks new ideas, alternative approaches and creative solutions; communication helps to ensure that the decisions made will support the best possible outcomes.

Here is an example that illustrates this process in action and the resulting magic for participants.

METHOD TO MAGIC

Diagnostic: You are organizing parent support groups for low-income, single-parent mothers. These mothers face significant challenges in getting to your sessions, e.g., transportation, child care, lack of motivation, feelings of being to blame and concerns about food.

Decisions: Create a participant-based organizing committee. Develop strategies with them to address these parents' unique challenges and to encourage attendance, e.g., build peer-group partnerships to support attendance – people will attend more regularly if they have a connection with others; provide transportation coupons free of charge; set up child care services on site; develop a reward system for participation, such as certificates; and offer snacks and a meal.

I felt important coming to this workshop – as if how I raised Michelle could make a real difference. They made an effort to make me feel comfortable – gave me free transportation and child care. I told them that mushrooms gave me indigestion and they took them off the menu. At other workshops I always felt as if the leader was doing me a favour by being there. I felt I was doing something wrong and she was correcting me. Not this time.

---

4. For further reading on the role of experience, imagination and reasoning, see Heirs, Ben and Peter Farrell, *The Professional Decision Thinker*. New York: Dodd, Mead and Co., 1987.

In this example, completing the diagnostic framework enables systematic, strategic decision making focused on finding appropriate tools and templates in Part II, and developing value-adds that are over and above client and participant expectations.

Choosing and Customizing Tools and Templates

Some facilitators/managers are concerned about using proven tips, tools and templates because their practice is focused on customized workshops where every session is distinct. Their argument is that tools and templates are too much like cookbook facilitation – they restrict creativity. For other facilitators/managers, tips, tools and templates spark their creativity. And they find it more efficient to build on something already tested rather than starting from scratch.

Although each workshop is unique, all workshops share some basic methods and requirements related to session management. The creativity and flair emerge as you set specifications, make decisions and then customize to suit. The time you save by avoiding routine tasks is time you can spend thinking about possibilities, sorting out issues and challenges, focusing on conceptual and creative work related to the quality of your session.

The most creative chefs in the world use tried and true methods to customize their favourite recipes. Leading fashion designers begin with basic principles about how to work with fabric and then create new designs within those parameters. Effective workshop management starts with a diagnostic framework that surfaces key decisions and challenges and enables effective decision making through the customization of selected tips, tools and templates.

Use the following criteria to assess which tips, tools or templates in Part II would support the management of your workshop.

Outcomes	Will this tip, tool or template track into workshop outcomes? Is your choice aligned with the longer-term outcomes desired by the client?
Culture	Does the template fit with the organizational culture?
People	Is the tool appropriate for this group of participants given their experience, level of expertise, learning needs, educational backgrounds?
Group Development	Does this tool fit the group's stage of development? Is this a mature group that has sorted out how they work together or are they meeting for the first time?
Facilitator Experience	Do you want to manage this workshop with a lot of control over the process and possible outcomes or are you comfortable dealing with whatever arises?
Ethno-cultural Considerations	Will a specific tool or management decision offend specific ethno-cultural groups in the workshop?
Literacy	Will the language in this tool fit with the language levels of participants?

Adding Value

A "value-add" is a positive and sometimes unexpected impact that can transform an ordinary experience into an exceptional experience. Value-adds are not included in contracts: they are over and above client and participant expectations.

> *Housing is a good example. As human beings we all need shelter. That basic need certainly falls into the physical level – a roof over our heads is necessary for survival against the elements. But if that house is also in a safe neighborhood, it adds security. Make it bigger and fancier, and comfort and enjoyment come into the mix along with the possible inclusion of status and satisfaction. Put this house on a lake or river or in the mountains, and also close to work, and it makes its way to aesthetic connection, maybe even peace. Now we're talking serious value. By impacting the consumer on multiple levels, you've gone from a basic need to a riot of worth that touches the entire being.* [5]

In workshop management, adding value is about keeping one question front and centre: in what ways can we optimize people's experiences at this workshop so that the outcome is magical for them?

One effective value-add is to provide clients with a draft electronic briefing note that they can send to workshop participants the day after a session is completed. Then participants can fine-tune the note and send it to their supervisors, team members or board of directors as an immediate report on the session.

The method in this value-add opportunity is to provide a quick, brief, efficient, informative workshop overview that supports effective communication and enables efficient reporting. The magic is that:

- it makes both the client and participants look good;
- participants can adapt the note to fit their situations;
- it supports your service goals as a workshop facilitator-manager.

---

5. LaSalle, Diana and Terry A. Britton. *Priceless: Turning Ordinary Products into Extraordinary Experiences*. Boston: Harvard Business School Press, 2003, p. 13. Adapted.

Develop value-adds based on the perspectives, context and orientation of your clients and participants. Look for this information in the results of your diagnostic framework under the following sections:

> Section 5: Participants,
>
> Section 6: Context, and
>
> Section 8: Best Scenario.

Customizing to preferences is key. Would group members think that your suggestion for quiet music during breaks is relaxing or flaky? Would music industry executives want some lively rock and roll after lunch or would they like to bring in their own CDs to play? Do lay church leaders in next month's religious retreat want some Buddhist chanting? How about financial services executives working on a recent cutback – do they want any music at all?

Workshop managers can add value to clients' and participants' experiences in a session in three key areas: participants, physical environment and information management.

Focus on participants

a. Use criteria to develop seating plans that mix participants according to their needs, e.g., whom they want to meet, what they want to learn.

b. Produce a participant list for post-event follow-up.

c. Carry a forget-me-not kit for every eventuality, e.g., reading glasses, tissues, Band-Aids, hand cream for dry hotel rooms where participants are handling a lot of paper, sticky notes to organize documents and ideas.

d. Provide unique giveaways that reinforce the workshop purpose, agenda, process or activity, e.g., mini-flashlights for shedding more light on a group's pet peeve.

e. Suggest strategies for following up with participants after the workshop in relation to key outcomes.

Focus on physical environment

a. In your pre-workshop needs assessment ask participants about special needs or preferences they may have in relation to menus, e.g., vegetarian food options, food sensitivities, allergies, accessibility.

b. For safety and security in risky areas, provide an escort to parking lots after dark.

c. Provide tantalizing, nutritious food and refreshments that are well presented and timed and that feature locally grown specialties and take-away recipes.

d. Provide comfortable chairs that turn and have wheels to enable optimal eye contact.

e. If microphones are required in a workshop with a round table format, provide one microphone per table to enable democratic participation. Two or three floor microphones for use in a large group restricts participation to those who are most comfortable speaking at a public microphone.

Focus on managing information

a. Develop a strategy for completing the workshop report in record time, e.g., within two days.

b. Provide a draft glossary of key terms and a list of acronyms in advance of the session. Then participants can review it at the workshop and suggest changes, additions, deletions for a final version to be included as an appendix in the workshop report.

c. Arrange for a video message at the workshop from an outstanding international leader in the area being discussed.

d. Ask participants what information they would like to have prior to the workshop in order to feel comfortable during discussions.

e. Provide presentation highlights in both hard copy and electronic versions so that participants can make their own notes during the presentation.

Adding value involves going beyond the basics to explore what you can do to enhance a workshop experience so that it is unexpectedly rich and rewarding. Every single value-add makes a difference. Cumulative value-adds multiply the positive impact of a session.

Conclusion

When it comes to setting up decision-making structures and processes, keep the structures simple and the processes customized. A minimalist, tailored approach to decision making enables ease of communication, creative value-adds and exceptional workshop experiences.

Part II

Tips, Tools and Templates

Introduction

The six chapters in Part II address key responsibility areas for workshop management. Tips, tools and templates in each chapter enable you to develop customized responses to the specifications and challenges identified in the diagnostic framework in Chapter 2, Part I.

    Chapter 4 – Participants

    Chapter 5 – Invitations

    Chapter 6 – Logistics, Locations and Layouts

    Chapter 7 – Speakers

    Chapter 8 – Handouts

    Chapter 9 – Feedback.

Tips are suggestions, key points and guiding principles based on experience and expertise.

Tools are handy checklists, approaches and short cuts – what works, based on successful practice.

Templates are patterns for constructing customized approaches. The templates in each chapter are on a disc on the back cover to enable quick customization. You just copy a template and adapt it to suit your situation.

Tips, tools and templates can:
- save time
- keep you on track
- enable consistency
- stimulate value-adds for clients
- provide a process outline
- encourage you to be more organized and efficient.

Chapter 4

Participants

★★★★★★★★★★★★★★★★★★★★★★★

★★★★★★★★★★★★★★★★★★★★★★★

Participants

People arrive at workshops along different paths: some come because they are eager to plan for the future; others because the session is mandatory; some want to meet interesting people; others are searching for answers to troubling situations.

Regardless of the paths participants take, it is primarily their presence and how they feel about being at a session that will determine the degree of success achieved. In this chapter we focus on what workshop managers/facilitators can do to ensure that the right participants are present in the right frame of mind to accomplish the workshop purpose and objectives.

This chapter provides tips, tools and templates for six areas of workshop management involving participants:

A. Types of Participation

B. Mix of Participants

C. Number of Participants

D. Observers

E. Participant Database

F. Participant Accessibility.

A. Types of Participation

Before writing a letter of invitation, creating a brochure, or thinking about who should be involved, ensure that the workshop organizing group takes a strategic look at which of the following five types of participation would best accommodate the session purpose and objectives: mandatory, invitational, restricted, open, or combination.

Mandatory

- Participants are designated to attend based on obligations, e.g., to an employer or supervisor, or through a contract or letter of agreement.

- Full participation throughout the workshop is expected, e.g., in discussions and small group activities.

- Workshop sponsors assume and hope that participants will take part in the workshop wholeheartedly based on good intentions and the potential for personal benefit and constructive outcomes, e.g., workplace safety for tree planting teams, babysitting certification programs.

- There is often an expectation related to implementation, e.g., follow through on recommendations or suggested action items.

Examples:
- a team development workshop for a police riot squad
- a facilitator training session for senior managers in the technology industry who are implementing a new performance management system.

Invitational

- Participants are invited to attend based on categories or criteria established by a planning committee in support of the workshop purpose and objectives.

- The invitation is designed to entice interested individuals who meet those criteria or are in those categories, e.g., a conflict management training program for union stewards, a session to develop national priorities for customer friendly electronic banking.

- Interested individuals who are not invited sometimes request an invitation; this request may be perceived by session organizers as an imposition and may not be granted, e.g., a workshop sponsor requests additional representation at a workshop where this would be viewed to be a conflict of interest.

- Participation throughout the workshop is motivated by anticipated benefits and potential impacts, e.g., to learn, to contribute to a field, to help shape an organization's future.

- The focus throughout the session is on the needs and interests of those invited, e.g., a pre-session questionnaire asks for participants' input on the agenda.

Examples:
- a time-management training program for truck drivers delivering perishable goods
- a session to develop provincial or state goals for literacy education
- a cardiopulmonary resuscitation (CPR) training session for new mothers.

Restricted

- A selected number of individuals is invited to attend a session for a specific reason.
- Participation is restricted and others are not permitted to request an invitation or to impose their participation on the session, e.g., the membership committee of a private golf course has a session on revising membership criteria with the assistance of an outside objective facilitator.
- Participants are predetermined by those with the power and influence to do so, or by the organization's mandate and bylaws.
- Participation in restricted sessions is often motivated by their urgency, privacy, exclusivity and solidarity, e.g., after the arrest of their Chief Executive Officer and Chief Financial Officer, the executive committee of a corporate board holds a one day session to update conflict-of-interest guidelines.
- Further mandatory, invitational or open workshops with larger numbers of participants often follow on the heels of restricted sessions, e.g., after the previous workshop with the executive committee, further sessions are held to explain and launch new company-wide conflict-of-interest guidelines.

Examples:
- a brainstorming session on new product business-case development for senior managers
- a board development workshop for directors of a global waste-management plan.

Open

- Participants are invited to attend based on the attractiveness of the opportunity, i.e., whether the topic, purpose and objectives meets their needs and interests or those of a group they represent.
- The workshop is available to all – there are no restrictions on who may attend.
- Participants determine if this is an appropriate workshop for them.

- Participation in workshop activities is based on a desire to contribute to or benefit from the purpose and objectives.

- Invitations often appear as announcements rather than letters and usually suggest who would be interested in the session.

Examples:
- a workshop on learning-centred approaches for university education is offered to professors and teaching assistants
- a session on managing diversity is offered to middle managers in corporations in a large urban environment.

Combination

- More than one type of participation is required to meet the workshop purpose, e.g., a product-marketing session that is mandatory for directors and supervisors, invitational to consumers and optional for staff.

- Customized communication is required for each type of participation, e.g., a mandatory media training session for Olympic coaches (which interested national athletes may also attend) requires clarity in relation to contracted responsibilities of coaches when interacting with the media; this information may not apply to interested athletes attending the session.

Examples:
- a corporate mission-development workshop that is mandatory for senior managers, invitational for marketing staff and optional for middle managers on the basis of interest
- a session on effective email communication that is offered as a result of an organization-wide survey; the workshop is mandatory (based on survey results) for middle managers and optional for other interested employees.

Participants

TIPS

✓ Before determining who needs to be present at a workshop, think about what **input, discussion and decision making** will be required when and by whom. Sometimes information can be gathered from a broad group of people in advance of the workshop so that a core group can work with this input during the session. Other times, mandatory attendance by all members of a team or organization is required at a workshop in order to meet the objectives.

METHOD TO MAGIC

Diagnostic: You are organizing a weekend invitational workshop for union representatives and their families on stress management. The event will be held at a beautiful resort. Educational day care will be provided. Union reps who have had time off for stress leave and others who have complained about stress-related illness are top priority for invitations. You are concerned that two friends of the union president have called twice to be invited.

Decisions: Although there is considerable pressure to include reps who have not experienced health issues related to stress management, the education coordinator for the union insists on maintaining his priority list, even when two reps who are close friends of the union president apply pressure to be invited.

This weekend was a huge step forward for our family. When my wife heard other reps talk about the pressures we all experience being caught between our members and company management, it was very comforting for her. She felt good spending time with other wives whose husbands work in the steel industry and who experience the same pressures on family as she does. Even our kids talked with other kids about being in union families. Only certain people were invited who had stress problems, so we were all in the same boat. No heroes – just us.

✓ Consider the following questions when making a decision about the type of participation best suited to a workshop:
  - How will this type of participation enable us to achieve our expected outcomes?
  - How does this decision reflect our values as a steering committee? For example, if we say that we are inclusive, how does our decision to restrict involvement to young women reflect that value?
  - Who is likely to support our decision to have this type of participation for this purpose and objectives? Who is not likely to support our decision to have this type of participation for this purpose and objectives? What are the implications of this support or lack of support for the long-term success of this initiative?

✓ Keep in mind that although workshop organizers are often clear about the type of participation they want, it is the participant who ultimately describes which type they experience.

> *" We ran an invitational workshop for several years on leadership development for senior executives. Each year, about 60% of participants attended voluntarily based on a desire to develop their leadership skills. About 40% were told to attend by their supervisors as a result of dissatisfaction with work performance. And about half of that 40% were clearly not pleased to be in a residential, week-long workshop on leadership skills. Their negativity had a real impact on the tone of discussions. "*

Participants in this workshop who came voluntarily would describe the type of participation as invitational to a specific category, i.e., senior executives. Others who were instructed to attend would say it was mandatory, as determined by their supervisors.

TOOL 4.1
WHAT'S YOUR TYPE?

Five types of participation are described below: mandatory, invitational, restricted, open and combination. Use these descriptions to answer the following question: given the purpose and objectives of this workshop, what type of participation would serve us best – mandatory, invitational, restricted, open, or some combination of these options?

Mandatory

Participants are designated to attend based on obligations, e.g., to an employer or supervisor, or through a contract or letter of agreement. Full participation throughout the workshop is required and participants are expected to engage wholeheartedly in discussions and small group activities. Proof of participation such as a signed registration form may be required, e.g., for academic credit or as part of a certification process.

Invitational

Participants are invited and encouraged to attend based on categories or criteria that support the workshop purpose and objectives and are endorsed by the sponsor and planning committee.

Restricted

A selected number of individuals is invited to attend a session for a specific reason tied to the purpose and objectives. Participation is restricted: others are not permitted to request an invitation or to impose their participation on the session.

Open

Participants are invited to attend based on the attractiveness of the opportunity, i.e., whether the topic or purpose and objectives meets their needs and interests, or those of a group they represent. The workshop is available to all – there are no restrictions on who may attend. The letter or announcement usually provides suggestions for who might be interested.

Combination

Some workshops require more than one type of participation to fulfill their objectives.

Decision

Type of Participation: _____

Rationale: _____

_____

_____

B. Mix of Participants

Getting the right mix of participants in a session is at the heart of what makes discussion and decision-making a meaningful experience. It is also what makes or breaks the success of a session in terms of outcomes over the long term.

Ensure that participants are invited or selected with the workshop purpose, objectives and agenda in mind. Set criteria for who should be invited or selected, using clear categories. The following categories are not finite – they overlap and interact. Customize them to suit your situation, ensuring that you avoid tokenism.[1]

Category	Examples
Affiliation	organization, department, unit, program, project, task force, team, committee, culture, religion, nationality
Authority	to make decisions, implement, follow through, lead, champion
Demography	age, gender, socio-economic status, education, health status, ethnicity, special needs
Expertise/Experience	generalist, specialist, consumer, veteran, newcomer
Geography	national, international, regional, state, provincial, municipal, local
Participation Skills	ability to communicate, be innovative, collaborate with others, manage conflict, think strategically, be creative
Perspectives	global, advocate, objective, supportive, critical
Position	executive director, chief executive officer, senior manager, volunteer, board member, staff member, elected representative, appointee, funder.

Depending on the type of workshop, the next step is to invite participants or announce the workshop in a way that enables the right people to attend. If the workshop is mandatory, you can develop an initial list of participants based on your criteria and then invite the people you have selected. If the workshop is open, you can announce it using existing avenues that will attract the kind of participants you want, e.g., in a targeted newsletter.

" The workshop was amazing just because of who was there. During one small group session I was sitting with our Global Vice-President of sales and two people from our Southeast Asia division. "

---

1. Tokenism: Granting minimal concessions, especially to minority or under-represented groups as a token gesture to appease radical demands, comply with legal requirements, etc. (Oxford Dictionary)

TIPS

✓ Well conceived workshops often generate lots of **interest and related pressures** to increase or change the participant list. Participants are the essence of a workshop. Their experience and collective wisdom will shape the outcomes of the process. Consider carefully all requests for additional participants.

Use your (a) diagnostic framework, (b) purpose and objectives, and (c) criteria for workshop participants as touchstones when your planning committee experiences these pressures and needs to make decisions.

> *" Clients often ask if other employees or students may attend workshops because they want to learn about facilitation or they would like to see how a design works, etc. Our general rule is to say "yes" in relation to conferences and seminars where the primary focus is on individual learning and relatively short educational sessions. We almost always say "no" to requests in relation to workshops, where a design has been developed to encourage group development and participants are expected to work collaboratively to achieve specific goals and objectives. "*

✓ When a workshop planning group is developing its initial participant list, consider the **type of participation** (i.e., mandatory, invitational, restricted, open, combination) and what categories of participants would contribute best to workshop outcomes. Then ask questions like the following to encourage clarification about who should be involved.

- What kinds of participants would make this workshop a real triumph? How have we appealed to them through this invitation or announcement?

- Do we have the right people at this session to ensure appropriate follow-up and implementation? What about advocacy groups who will not be involved in implementation if they aren't involved in the decision-making process at this session?

- How would this particular individual contribute to our purpose?

- Which objective(s) do you see that person addressing?

- It looks as if he is in the "big picture" generalist category. Do we need more people in that category or should we be looking for more participants in the technical expertise or specialist category?

- Sometimes it's better to have people in the tent than outside of it criticizing what is going on inside. Can you think of anyone whom we need to bring inside the tent?

METHOD TO MAGIC

Diagnostic: You are organizing a restricted and confidential 1.5 day summit for partners in your large legal firm. The purpose of the summit is to decide how to develop and implement a mandatory retirement package for aging partners.

Decisions: Invite the managing partner and his direct reports. Include three outside human resources consultants to provide creative expertise as problem solvers. Invite two retired partners who have already experienced mandatory retirement in the firm. Involve outside experts and retired partners during the first half-day.

The right people were in the room to get this job done. We heard from experts in the field of early retirement. Then we spent time talking with partners in our firm who had already experienced this. Then it was our turn. We had to translate our firm's values into a program that wouldn't alienate current partners. It wasn't easy, but it worked – and we had lots of real life experience in the room to make it happen.

- ✓ Sometimes workshops have a group of **preferred participants** who are their top priority, and then other groups whom they will welcome if they can't get everyone they want from the primary group. For example, you may prefer to have only experienced facilitators in a training session on group development but decide that you will take people who have related experience if space is available.

- ✓ When you have set your criteria for participation and have a limited number of places, choose participants who wear **more than one hat**, e.g., a female leader from a western state or province who is a dynamic change agent and also has a lot of experience and expertise in the topic area: eight hats.

- ✓ If you want to hold a workshop but don't have a list of **potential participants**, consider asking a small core group of four or five colleagues or community members to suggest three or four other people who might want to become involved. In this way you build a list through referrals and also initiate communication and coalition building.

> *You are one of an initial core group of invitees to this workshop. We would like to have about 30 experienced teachers from diverse disciplines as participants in this session. Please provide by return email the names of two teachers outside of your subject area who you think would be interested in attending this workshop and collaborating with colleagues from across the country to achieve the purpose stated previously. For each recommended participant, please provide:*
> - *Name, current position, phone, email*
> - *Experience/expertise/qualities this person could contribute to the purpose of this workshop.*

✓ Many workshops have **"secondary" participants** and related objectives, i.e., those who are not present in the session but who will benefit from or need to be involved in the workshop outcomes. When you are developing your participant list, make sure you keep linkages to and communication with secondary participants in mind, e.g., who will be present at the workshop and can communicate with secondary participants in her area of interest?

✓ In some situations, an organizing committee does not want to get involved in the **politics of individual participant selection.** In these situations, develop a list of organizations that fit your criteria and request that the organization name a delegate. If you have someone specific in mind whom you would like an organization to send, you may want to have an initial phone conversation with an organizational leader in which you express your request verbally before sending a formal invitation.

✓ A common question that arises is whether participants should attend as **representatives of their organizations or based on expertise or some combination.** The answer to this question lies in the purpose of the workshop. Organizational representatives bring their organization's perspective and authority to discussions, whereas experts bring individual knowledge, understanding and experience in relation to a specific topic.

Sometimes a participant brings both representation and expertise to a session. When this is the case, it is important to determine whether this person's comments reflect his organization's stance or individual opinion, as the answer to this question can have a significant impact on how his input is viewed by others in the workshop and on what decisions are made.

Many workshops provide expertise through speakers, background research and surveys so that individuals representing participating organizations can use this information for decision-making purposes. In situations where an objective facilitator has been hired in support of an unbiased process, it is important that both participants and invited speakers represent a fair range of perspectives or the process will lose its objectivity.

Part II: Tips, Tools and Templates

Tool 4.2

Participant Mix

This tool enables workshop organizers to think systematically about the kinds of participants who would work best together in a session.

Review the following list of eight potential categories for participants and select the ones that are relevant to the purpose and objectives of your session. These categories are not finite – they overlap and interact. Customize them to suit your situation. Decide on a general percentage or number of participants for each of the categories you have selected, e.g., you may decide that 100% of participants should have the authority to make decisions and that you need a good gender balance. Depending on the nature of the workshop, a gender balance may be 50% male teachers and 50% female teachers or 90% female nurses and the rest male or 98% male welders and the rest female.

Category	% or #	Names
Affiliation, e.g., organization, department, unit, program, project, task force, team, committee, culture, religion, nationality		
Authority, e.g., to make decisions, implement, follow through, lead, champion		
Demography, e.g., age, gender, socio-economic status, education, health status, ethnicity, special needs		
Expertise/Experience, e.g., generalist, specialist, consumer, veteran, newcomer		
Geography, e.g., national, international, regional, state, provincial, municipal		
Participation Skills, e.g., communicating, innovating, collaborating, managing conflict, thinking strategically, being creative		
Perspectives, e.g., neutral, supportive, critical, global, advocate		
Position, e.g., executive director, chief executive officer, senior manager, volunteer, board member, staff, elected representative, appointee, funder		
Other (specify) *Language (FR & ENG)*		

72

TOOL 4.3
DO WE HAVE THE RIGHT PARTICIPANTS?

Review the following questions with your participant list in mind, noting areas where you need to think about additional changes.

- For each of the workshop objectives, name one or two participants who you think are able to make a substantive contribution to achieving the objective.

  _____

- How do the workshop objectives meet the needs of those who are coming?

  _____

- When you look at the group as a whole, what do you think the tone of the workshop will be? Why? Is this what you want?

  _____

- Do you have people with the right kinds of power and influence required to make this workshop successful, e.g, expertise, influence in decision making and implementation. For each type of power, name one or two participants who bring this capacity.

  _____

- Who is coming to the session who might be described as "a breath of fresh air"?

  _____

- To what extent is this list inclusive or exclusive? What effect will your answer have on the long-term impact of this workshop?

  _____

- Do you have at least three distinct perspectives represented at the session? Name these perspectives and how they link to your objectives.

  _____

- When you think about the outcomes of this workshop, is there an "in" or "out" crowd in the participant list? If "yes," what is the potential impact on the outcomes you want?

  _____

- Will this group provide you with the energy required to support the workshop process, plenary and small group discussions and decision making?

  _____

- Which participants have a commitment to implementation?

  _____

Part II: Tips, Tools and Templates

Tool 4.4

Participant Matrix for a National Research Summit

Participant Matrix

	First Name	Last Name	Organization	Content Expertise	A. Criteria: Academia / Basic Biomedical / Clinical / Health Systems and Services / Knowledge Transfer/Capacity Building Expertise	B. Affiliation: Consumer / Non-Governmental Organizations / Clinicians, e.g., physicians, nurses / International Representation	C. Other: Province/Territory / Gender / Planning Committee Member / Reference Group Member	COMMENTS
1								
2								
3								
4								
5								
6								
7								
8								
9								
10								
11								
12								
13								
14								
15								
16								
17								
18								
19								
20								

Conclusions: _____

C. Number of Participants

When it comes to workshops, bigger isn't necessarily better – too many or too few participants can spoil the process.

TIPS

✓ Use the Workshop Diagnostic Framework in Chapter 2 to determine the **optimal number of participants** required to support the purpose, objectives and type of session.

- What is the smallest number of participants that will enable you to achieve expected outcomes within a positive process?

- What is the largest number of participants you can have and still achieve expected outcomes within a positive process?

When the number of participants in a workshop increases, the process tends to take longer. There is also the risk that the workshop will become more like a conference, where the focus is on learning in a large group.

✓ If your **objectives** are partly to have a conference focused on learning and partly to have a workshop focused on planning, consider having an initial day that is a conference and has a larger number of participants followed by a second day focused on action planning that has fewer participants.

✓ There is often **pressure to add participants** for reasons not directly related to the workshop purpose, e.g.,
  - they are in town for another event
  - they would give presentations free of charge
  - they are friends of other participants or members of the planning committee
  - an influential supporter of the workshop wants to "return" an invitation to a colleague who invited her to participate in a previous session.

Stand firm on your decisions as a planning committee when it comes to questions about adding participants, i.e., what you concluded in the workshop diagnostic framework and what criteria you set to guide participant selection or invitation.

> *" Our last planning committee meeting was a real doozy. I thought we had completed the list of participants. At our previous session we had all agreed on criteria and had invited a solid list of 45 people. And then suddenly, at this meeting, two committee members wanted to add eight additional people who were friends of theirs and who they openly said should be included because they had been invited out-of-state to these individuals' events in the past.*
>
> *I was floored, and not just because this kind of thing perpetuates the same people going to all the same meetings and pushing the same agendas. But because eight more people means another round table, more space, food and kits – and the location and our budget just can't handle this.*
>
> *It was a tough discussion – lots of politics involved. Eventually we decided to stick with the initial list and to send a special letter to these eight individuals informing them about the workshop and asking them if they would participate in a telephone interview as part of the background information package. That way we could give them some profile and learn from their experience without compromising the process. "*

✓ After deciding on the number of participants, select a **venue** that is slightly larger than what you need so that if you do end up with a larger group you will be able to accommodate them.

D. Observers

Questions about the appropriateness of observers or participant-observers often come up when planning a workshop. Observers are fine during conferences and seminars, when the numbers are large and their presence is less noticeable. During workshops, the presence of observers can often complicate the process.

TIPS

✓ Clarify exactly what you mean by the term **"observer."** Is this person not to participate in any way, or in some ways but not others? The more clarity you bring to this discussion, the more comfortable the observer and other participants will be in the workshop.

- If an observer is to take notes on small group discussions and then report in plenary, be clear that he is to be objective and that people can't involve him in discussions.

- If someone is observing a workshop on organizational values, will he sit outside the workshop group, thus ensuring that he doesn't participate in the session? How will he interact with other participants during breaks and meals, e.g., will he be allowed to discuss his perspective with participants?

- If a vice-president wants to observe a half-day workshop on issues analysis with a group managed by one of her direct reports, what exactly does she mean by "observe"? What impact will this have on people's ability to disclose concerns and discuss them openly? How will the person who is the direct report feel in this situation?

✓ When thinking about involving the **media**, consider all possible angles. If they are observing and taking notes at a workshop, keep in mind that they will report on what they find potentially "interesting" to readers.

Representatives of the media are usually welcome at conferences involving expert speakers and general discussions where they report on research and new perspectives. On the other hand, they are commonly excluded from decision-making sessions that bring together disparate views through collaborative processes that may seem quite contentious to outsiders, but are a necessary part of building agreement. The central consideration is whether you want these intense discussions reported in the media or whether you would prefer to announce the results of the discussions through a press release or some other mechanism.

✓ Clarify exactly what you mean by the term **"participant-observer."** Does this person provide specific information on request but not participate in discussions or try to influence decision making?

A participant-observer role may be requested for staff at an annual general meeting (AGM) for members of a professional association. In this situation, staff are not permitted to vote or to influence discussion; they are present only in their capacity as experts on specific questions. Thus they participate by providing information but observe when it comes to discussion and decision making.

✓ **Avoid having observers and/or participant-observers present** at workshops when:
- the content of the workshop is personal or confidential and you want people to feel comfortable speaking candidly about their experiences and understandings without feeling watched, e.g., a team development workshop on how to address harassment issues in the workplace

  > *Sometimes we have team-building workshops that are designed to address issues. In these sessions the subject matter is intensely personal and involves people in confrontation and deep emotion, so we do not have observers or other participants present who are not on the immediate team, e.g., an observer or representative from the human resources department. Having others present, regardless of their goodwill and skill, jeopardizes the confidentiality that is necessary to build effective relationships. It is also likely to guarantee that the real issues will not be addressed openly and candidly*

- the workshop tasks challenge participants to explore new ideas and practise skills, e.g., senior managers learn how to provide feedback to employees on competency challenges
- the workshop purpose is to develop a plan or advocacy strategy that must be kept secret from competitors or opposing groups
- the purpose of the workshop is to make final decisions based on research and evidence in controversial topic areas, e.g., a national consensus-building workshop on environmental research priorities in support of increased fish stock.

✓ **A client may want to observe** (rather than participate in) an internal organizational workshop to ensure that his goals are being met — a fair request, particularly if the client is funding the workshop.

Clarify how this could happen:

- Does the client want to be introduced at the beginning and then observe for a short time, returning at the end of the workshop?
- Does he want to come in periodically to see how things are going? How would this affect participation?

✓ Once you have made a decision about observers, agree on how you will respond to **pressures to change** that decision.

> *" Our steering committee discussed the pros and cons of having observers present and decided that, given the purpose of the seminar, we would restrict this particular meeting to team members only. We also agreed not to make any exceptions to this decision. "*

Tool 4.5

Observers – Yes or No?

Use the following questions to explore with your workshop planning committee whether you want to have observers (or participant-observers) in a workshop.

- How are we defining observers/participant-observers? In what ways and to what extent will these people be observers/participant-observers?

- What do we stand to gain in terms of our purpose and objectives through having observers/participant-observers in the workshop? What do we stand to lose?

- What are potential positive and negative impacts on workshop participants of having observers/participant-observers present?

- How difficult will it be for people to maintain the role of observer/participant-observer given the workshop process and their potential to contribute to outcomes?

- Will our decision about observers/participant-observers in this workshop set a precedent for future sessions? How comfortable are we with our response to this question?

E. Participant Database

A comprehensive and efficient participant database saves time, creates customized records and provides you with an updating mechanism for reports to clients.

TIPS

✓ A participant database needs to fit the **purpose and objectives** of the workshop. If one objective is to build a network, you may want to ask participants what information they would like to see included in a network database, and then build it based on what they say, e.g., include information about educational backgrounds and research interests.

✓ Include a **checklist option** in your database so that you can record where you are on specific milestones, e.g., registrations received, hotel bookings completed, pre-session packages sent out.

✓ Check your country's **privacy laws**. Canada has legislation (Bill C-6) that outlines specific guidelines in this area.

✓ Check your **client's privacy policies:** they may require you to do things in a specific way, e.g., some organizations do not publish home phone numbers or email addresses due to harassment considerations; some professional associations do not publish email addresses in an effort to prevent members of the public from seeking free advice of members; some corporations are only publishing electronic addresses to support reduced use of paper communication.

✓ Ask participants if they are comfortable having their **coordinates published** in a list of participants or in the workshop report or provided on request to other organizations with similar interest areas.

The following question appears on many registration forms:

> *May we include your coordinates (name, address, email address, telephone numbers) in the participant list and report for this conference?*
>
> *Yes* __ *No* __ *Partial* __ *(see below)*
>
> *Please include only:*
>
> _____
>
> _____

✓ Look for opportunities such as the following to contribute **value-adds** for both your client and participants when you create your database:

- create the database in a program and format that your client finds easy to use
- provide your client with a sample list of categories and ask if he would like any additional features
- explore whether your workshop database has value to other interested parties, e.g., groups in another geographical location with similar interests
- explore whether your client and participants would appreciate receiving databases of other sessions or groups who have similar interests. Remember to get permission prior to sharing databases.

TOOL 4.6
DATABASE CHECKLIST

Circle numbers on the following checklist for items that you want to include in your participant database.

1. name
2. accessibility concerns (see section F of this chapter)
3. title
4. organization
5. position
6. address – home
7. address – business
8. phone – home
9. phone – business
10. fax
11. email address
12. Web site
13. pager number
14. educational degrees
15. publications
16. affiliations
17. areas of interest related to the workshop purpose
18. workshop role, e.g., speaker, committee member, participant
19. questions they are currently exploring in the workshop topic area
20. a publication recommended to other participants
21. food allergies and preferences
22. hotel room requirements
23. other: _____

Template 4.7
Participant Database Information

Name of Event:

Participant's Name:

Title/Position:

Organization (if applicable):

Address for courier delivery:

Telephone No: Fax No: Email:

Preferred method for receiving background information: Mail ___ Fax ___ Email ___

Meeting materials will be in English. Do you require French or Spanish translation?

Yes ____   No ____

The proceeding of the Forum will be conducted in English. Do you require simultaneous translation?

Yes ____   No ____

May we include all or part of your coordinates (address, email, telephone number, etc.) in the participant list and report for this meeting?

Yes ____   No ____   Part only (please specify details) _____

Meeting Requirements:

We want to ensure that you have as pleasant an experience as possible at the workshop. Please indicate any special dietary or other requirements.

Dietary: _____

Other: _____

Accommodation Requirements:

Do you require accommodation? Yes ___ No ___

Duration of stay (dates and time of arrival): Check in _____   Check out _____

Credit Card for Incidental Expenses: Name on card _____

Type: _____   Number _____   Expiry _____

Special room requirements (if any): _____

F. Participant Accessibility

Persons with disabilities who participate in a workshop have a right to full involvement to the greatest extent possible.[2] Acting on this right means ensuring that workshops are based on the values of equity, inclusion and independence, as outlined in the following questions:

- How can you ensure that persons with disabilities have **equitable access** to all aspects of the workshop experience?

- How can you set up your workshop to support the **full participation and inclusion** of persons with disabilities?

- What can you do to enable persons with disabilities to be **independent** in your workshop?[3]

TIPS

✓ Check **relevant values, policies, laws and agreements** (in your municipality, region, province, state, country) related to accessibility as they may require specific action for compliance.

✓ Ask your client for his **organizational policies and programs** related to accessibility so that you can ensure that the workshop is aligned with organizational values.

✓ Use the **workshop registration form** to find out about special needs participants may have, e.g.,

> *We want to ensure that you have as pleasant an experience as possible at the conference. Please indicate any special dietary, room or other requirements that we should know about.*

---

2. For more information on Canadian approaches to disability issues, see the Web site of the Office for Disability issues, Human Resources Development Canada, Government of Canada: www.hrdc-drhc.gc.ca. The Canadian Constitution, in its section on equality under the Canadian Charter of Rights and Freedoms states: 15.(1) "Every individual is equal before and under the law and has the right to equal protection and equal benefit of the law without discrimination and, in particular without discrimination based on race, national or ethnic origin, colour, religion, sex, age or mental or physical disability."

3. Ibid. "The Government of Canada has a vision of an inclusive society, one in which all Canadians have the opportunity to participate fully and enjoy the benefits and responsibilities of citizenship. The 1999 Speech from the Throne clearly sets out the Government of Canada's commitment to work with "other governments, the private and voluntary sectors, and all citizens to build communities in which Canadians with disabilities are fully included."

✓ Think about a **wide range of special needs** related to access – from those that are simple and easy to accommodate to those that are more complex, e.g.,
  - some participants may need a site that enables good cell phone reception for emergencies
  - some participants may require a guarantee that no food will touch any peanut products; others may require gluten-free or vegetarian menus;
  - some participants may prefer windows that open; others may be allergic to tobacco smoke or perfume.

✓ For more complex situations, use the following **Participant Accessibility Map (PAM)** template in this chapter to enable you to address a participant's requirements.

✓ When using PAM with participants, **communicate** with them regularly to let them know that you are keeping their needs in the forefront.

✓ Use PAM to find out ahead of time if participants have **special needs related to room set-up**:
  - some people with hearing disabilities need to sit where they can see everyone in the room so that they can read lips
  - others who have hearing aids may ask to sit away from flip charts so that the noise of turning pages doesn't interfere with their hearing devices
  - individuals with joint problems may require seating that has increased support
  - persons experiencing problems with anxieties may prefer to sit in certain areas of the room, e.g., close to an exit
  - people using wheelchairs will need enough space to be comfortable when seated at tables or next to other participants.

✓ Take the time to **put yourself in the position** of a person with a disability who is coming to a session. Let's take the example of someone with muscular dystrophy who uses a wheelchair. First try to visualize the challenges she faces on a day-to-day basis.

Then visualize how she will travel to the workshop location; register at the hotel; travel to the site; enter the building; pick up her registration package; enter the workshop room; approach and take a seat; read handouts; move into small groups; manage the buffet lunch you have planned; get to washroom, oxygen if it is required or off-site social functions.

✓ Contact appropriate levels of government to find out what **grants and services** they provide in support of access for persons with disabilities, e.g.,

- Will your municipal government fund a caregiver for a person with special needs?

- Does your provincial or state government have a program focused on increasing accessibility to workshops, courses or programs?

The recipe for building a positive and supportive workshop environment for participants with disabilities is based on mindfulness – keeping in mind accessibility in its broadest sense so that you make thoughtful decisions grounded in the values of equity, inclusion and independence.

✓ Once you have named the requirements, identify how you will **follow through**, e.g.,

- Where can you get signers for individuals who are deaf?

- Which hotels are accessible to people in wheelchairs?

- Can you provide Braille handouts?

✓ Some participants require an assistant – perhaps a person who is already allocated to work with the facilitator. Introduce this person as a **"room assistant"** available to assist with special needs, e.g., if medication(s) must be taken at a specific time, please let the room assistant know so that he or she can remind you at the correct time; have the room assistant available to assist with refreshments and buffet-style breaks.

> *" Believe it or not, being on your own can be a stressful feature for disabled people who, unlike me, might not be outgoing and might not like to attend functions where they do not already know someone. Also, many unlikely participants utilize this support, e.g., a woman asked for a reminder nod as she had to telephone her child's principal at a pre-arranged time. "*

Template 4.8

Participant Accessibility Map[4]

Participant:	How Travelling:
Arrival Date:	Departure Date:

Check items that are of concern:

Mobility: ____ Vision: ____ Hearing: ____ Speech: ____ Dexterity: ____

Health Condition: *See specifics on next page*

Participant uses:
(mark "B" if you will bring your own or "P" if it must be provided on site)

__ Wheelchair (see specifics next page)   __ Attendant/care provider
__ Scooter (see specifics next page)   __ Dialysis
__ Wheelchair access/room accommodations   __ ASL sign language
__ Wheelchair access/transport assistance   __ Hearing aid(s)
__ Shower chair   __ TDD (telephone device/deaf)
__ Raised toilet seat   __ Portable FM amplifier
__ Bath safety bars   __ Bliss communication board
__ Crutches, canes or foldable walker   __ Flashing/vibrating fire alarms
__ Prosthesis: arm(s) or leg(s)   __ Reads via: Braille __ Audiocassette __
__ Oxygen concentrator   Enlarged Text __
__ Oxygen cylinders   __ Guide dog
__ Hoyer lift device for transferring   __ Prescribed medications
__ Elevator or escalator   *(list under Health Conditions next page)*
__ Breathing ventilator: full-time ventilator __   part-time c-pap ventilator __
                  part-time bi-pap ventilator __

Other: _____

IMPORTANT: *Oxygen must be pre-arranged with all carriers and points of distribution.*

Personal Transportation

Type: Wheelchair __   Scooter: __   **Manufacturer's Name:** _____

Client uses: full-time __   part-time __   client-owned __   client-rented __

Other Features: foot rests __   backpack __   basket __   caneholder __
          removable arm(s) __   dismantles into __ number of pieces

Type: Manual __ Electric __   **# of Batteries** ___   **Type of Batteries:** Gel __ Acid __

Electrical charger plug: 3 prong North American volts __   Plug adapter needed __

---

4. This template is an adaptation of "Client Accessibility Profile" developed by Susan Wheeler and reprinted here with permission of the publisher. Susan is a Canadian advocate for people with disabilities – particularly those with Charcot-Marie-Tooth (CMT) disease – and is the editor of CMT Today magazine: cmt.today@sympatico.ca.

Weight: _____ Height: _____ Width: _____ Length: _____

Health Conditions
1. Prescribed Medications

Drug Name	Dosage	Reason for Taking

Refrigeration needed: Yes ___   No ___

Other Assistance: _____

2. Dietary Requirements

Diabetic ___ Gluten-Free ___ Vegetarian ___ Lactose-Free ___ Low fat (heart diet) ___

Comments/Details: _____

_____

Food Allergies (please list): _____

_____

3. Other Required Treatments or Assistance
(e.g., blood pressure checks)

_____

_____

_____

Client wears MEDI-ALERT identification: Yes ___   No ___
Remarks noted on: Bracelet ___   Necklace ___   in case of loss:

Part II: Tips, Tools and Templates

Physician Information

Official medical documentation from physician provided: Yes __   No __
Date provided: _____

Family Physician's Name and Address: _____

_____

_____

Telephone No: _____   Fax No: _____   Email: _____

Emergency Contacts

Contact #1: Name and Address	Contact #2: Name and Address
Telephone No:	Telephone No:
Fax No:	Fax No:

Other Relevant Information

_____

_____

Agreement* — *Please read and sign.*

Client

Any and all personal information provided within this Participant Accessibility Map is provided voluntarily. I further release any and all the provided information to workshop organizers, the travel agent and their agent representative(s), who, on my behalf, will make every effort to coordinate the special care services and/or the accessible accommodations I require. In addition to this, I fully understand and agree that the said named workshop organizers, the travel agent and their agent representative(s) cannot be held liable should any accessibility and/or special care services:

- Not be provided by workshop organizers, carriers or points of destinations
- Not meet with pre-travel accessibility/special care service guarantees
- Cause any negative health or well-being ramifications during and post workshop sessions and travel.

Workshop Manager

Any and all information provided within this Participant Accessibility Map will be used for the sole purpose of coordinating accessible workshop site accommodations and/or coordinating special care services for the above-named client while travelling. Relevant information may/will be forwarded to workshop organizers, site managers, travel carriers and to points of destinations to (a) enquire about and (b) confirm accessibility/special care service requirements.

Signature: _____   Signature: _____

Date: _____   Date: _____

* Note: This is a sample agreement only and should be reviewed with a legal advisor to ensure its appropriateness for your jurisdiction.

Chapter 5

Invitations

★ ★

★ ★

Invitations

The workshop starts when the anticipation starts – with the first contact that potential participants have with those organizing a session. This communication may be through a letter, an announcement, an advertisement in a newspaper or a phone call from a friend or colleague. Invitations and announcements appear in a broad range of formats, lengths and approaches: they may be a formal letter of several paragraphs, a simple brochure, or a brief, well designed email piece that looks like a party invitation.

Regardless of the purpose or type of workshop you are managing, the time you spend crafting a letter or announcement can have major returns in both registration numbers and the initial attitudes of participants.

This chapter provides tips, tools and templates for you to customize when creating written, verbal, hard copy and electronic invitations, announcements and related items such as letters of support. There are three main sections:

A. Letters and Announcements

B. International Requirements

C. Challenging Situations.

This chapter does not include registration forms or marketing strategies for workshops, e.g., brochures, flyers or distribution mechanisms, as these aspects of workshop organization are usually handled by individuals with professional expertise in this area. See the Association of Meeting Planners or Meeting Planners International for more information.

A. Letters and Announcements

When the subject of letters or announcements comes up, clients invariably ask, "Do you have a sample I could have a look at?" or "With your experience, you could probably write this in no time at all – how about doing a first draft?" This request usually happens because those responsible for the session recognize the influence that the letter or announcement may have on who will register for a session and how they will participate.

This influence is the result of three key elements in invitations: persuasion, information and engagement – the PIE formula:

To get the right proportions of a workshop PIE, think about the needs, interests and perspectives of workshop participants (see the Diagnostic Framework in Chapter 2), and ask yourself the following questions.

Persuade

- Do you need to encourage potential participants to sign up, e.g., through special incentives or an appeal to the benefits of professional education?

- Do you want to convince the executive director of an organization to send a number of representatives to a workshop during a particularly busy time of year?

- Do potentially cynical participants need to start thinking constructively about a mandatory and likely tense Issues Analysis Workshop?

TIPS

✓ Create a positive first impression. Catch the respondent's eye in both hard copy and electronic versions through the **credibility** of your letterhead, logo, and whom the letter is coming from.

> *As Crown Attorney for our region, I am delighted to sponsor your participation in the upcoming workshop on the cost-benefit analysis of alternative justice systems.*

✓ Be strategic about **how you invite** participants. Do you want potential participants to make their decision about attending based on a written or verbal invitation? Renowned participants and speakers often prefer to be approached in person or by phone (prior to receiving a written invitation) as an indication of the importance of their involvement and status in an area.

✓ Think about **staging** your invitations or announcements. Do you want an advance invitation to a selected group of "must have" participants followed by a slightly later invitation to a broader group?

✓ Be **transparent** about the invitation process for the workshop.

> *An initial invitation is being sent to 25 individuals selected by the steering committee based on their success in this area over the past year. Two weeks after this invitation is issued a general announcement will be made on the Web and registrations will be accepted on a "first-come first-served" basis to a maximum of 60 participants.*

METHOD TO MAGIC

Diagnostic: You are inviting participants to a two-day memoir-writing workshop to be held in a beautiful, heritage church in your community. Anyone who is interested can attend. The workshop leader is a renowned historian and writer who has published several successful historical mystery novels and is now ghost-writing the memoirs of a recent Giller Prize author. Space in the church hall is limited to 44 participants with four people per round table.

Decisions: Develop an announcement that appeals to writers first and then to historians. Create the announcement based on a PIE formula that focuses mostly on persuasion in relation to the development and improvement of writing skills. Include basic logistical information about date, time, location, lunch, cost, registration. Engage participants before the session by asking them to read and bring with them a memoir that they like.

Publish the announcement about the workshop in two phases: first to church members, one of whom initiated the idea and booked the hall at minimal cost, and then two weeks later to the historical society and other potentially interested organizations in the community.

I was keen on going to this session as soon as I saw the title in the church bulletin – "Writing Delicious Memoirs." For several years now I have been thinking about recording what it's like to live the life of a "thalidomide baby" and how awful that expression is. This seemed like a non-threatening but exciting way to get started. Someone told me about the well-known writer who was leading it and his gentle personality and that clinched it. I was the third person to sign up.

✓ Persuade potential participants about the benefits of expected outcomes by emphasizing how the workshop results could or will be **implemented.**

✓ Be clear about the **purpose** and expected **outcomes** of the workshop and how participants stand to benefit from attending.

> *Our agenda is clear: we need to get our issues on the table and create ways to address them. And we need to do that in a mutually respectful and supportive environment.*
>
> *We're good at this - this is what our video production company is known for. The process is familiar and so are the players - let's make this team development event our best one ever.*

Inform

- What information do potential participants need to make arrangements, e.g., date, location, time, how to register?

- What basic information (e.g., purpose, objectives, who is being invited) will help people decide whether this workshop is for them?

- What do potential participants need to know about expenses, e.g., registration fees, travel and accommodation expenses and who is paying for what?

If you are announcing an internal mandatory team development workshop, your announcement might **inform** participants briefly about how the need for the session became apparent and when and where it will be held; include documents that provide background information for discussions, then **persuade** them to think positively about the session by discussing benefits to them and their divisions; and finally ask them to **engage** their colleagues in some preliminary discussions about key issues to be discussed.

TIPS

✓ When **creating an invitation,** start with the workshop diagnostic framework (Chapter 2). Ask yourself what information someone needs to make a decision about whether or not to attend a workshop or to have a positive attitude about a session. Then put that information in the invitation or announcement.

✓ Avoid references to **vague sources** such as:
  - recent research indicates ...
  - leading experts agree that ...
  - a national poll recently indicated that ...

✓ Avoid using your initial contact with participants to **overload** them with too much information (TMI) that could be distributed later.

✓ Be clear about whether the workshop **purpose and objectives are in final or in draft form**.

✓ If possible, send out the letter or announcement far enough in advance that potential participants have time to book the event in their schedules. **Rushed timelines** can be irritating and reduce the importance of the session in the eyes of participants.

✓ If there are concerns about **liability,** address them.

> *The Organizing Committee will not assume any responsibility for damage or injuries to persons or property during the Conference. It is recommended that participants and accompanying persons arrange for personal travel and health insurance.*

✓ Give **privacy**[1] some consideration. Ask participants if they are comfortable having their coordinates published in a list of participants or in the workshop report or made available to other organizations with similar interest areas. Asking permission is a form of persuasion. Permission marketing leaves the decision with the purchaser.

---

1. See Chapter 2 for more information on privacy laws and policies.

✓ **Clothing** can be a source of anxiety to workshop participants who may prefer to be comfortable but worry about being dressed inappropriately. In situations where you want to reduce this stress, provide a general guideline for dress:

- *Dress is business casual.*

- *This workshop is being held at our Corporate Training Centre where a dress code of business casual applies except in the fitness centre. Our session on Tuesday evening will be held at the National Arts Centre where participants are asked to dress more formally for dinner and the following concert.*

OR

- *In the interests of personal comfort and creativity, please dress casually. The setting is very informal, with denim acceptable for dinner.*

✓ Have a clear **cancellation policy.**

Notification of cancellation must be made in writing to the Workshop Coordinator. Payments regarding registration fees, hotel accommodation, social programs and tours will be refunded as follows:

- *full refund minus handling fee of $100 by (date)*
- *no refund if cancellation after (date)*
- *financial credits are not given for late arrivals, unused services or unattended events*
- *all refunds will be processed within one month after the conference*
- *registrants are encouraged to take out travel insurance as well as insurance that covers costs related to cancellation due to health or other unpredictable causes.*

Engage

- How can you engage participants in the subject areas to be discussed, e.g., by providing statistics, by making relationships between their personal and professional lives and the workshop topic, by pointing to local, regional, national and global implications related to the workshop topic?

- What could participants do to prepare for the session, e.g., read background information, consult with colleagues?

- How could participants explore broader issues related to the workshop topic, e.g., look on your Web site, in books, in recent news articles, on upcoming radio and television programs?

TIPS

✓ Engage potential participants through **first impressions**. In the first few seconds that people read your invitation, they are making judgments about the workshop and whether it will fit their needs and interests. They are forming opinions about whether other participants will have similar backgrounds, work histories, educational profiles, publications, practical skills. They are wondering what personal benefits they will get in addition to the stated workshop purpose: Will they encounter people with similar commitment at a community or global level? Will they meet people who can enable an advantageous career move? Will they be able to share and gain insights that they can't realize in their home settings?

✓ To make a **positive first impression** with participants, consider the following questions.

- What tone do you want convey in your invitation:
    - formal or informal?
    - academic or non-academic?
    - warm or cool?
    - loosely or highly organized?
    - relaxed and laid back or highly focused and urgent?
    - technical or artistic?
    - thoughtful or impetuous?
    - other: _____

- Do you need some power and influence to get the right people in the room? If so, how can you convey that kind of support in your invitation, e.g., through who signs it?

- Will a letter or announcement suffice or do you need to start with an invitation by phone or in person and then follow it up with something written?

✓ **Hook your respondent** in the first few sentences, as the Vice-President of Sales in a multinational technology company did in a note about a mandatory session with account managers.

> *I need your help. It's national account planning time and the information we need to meet our goals for next year is all in your heads. It's time for us to share some of that data with each other so that we can cook up a strategy that plugs us into another A1 Club year. Next year's A1 Club event is 10 days in Singapore – all expenses paid. Let's work it so that we can be there together.*

✓ Be strategic about **how fancy** you want your invitation to look. Will recipients prefer a full colour, hard copy letter of invitation or a simpler email announcement linked to a Web site or both?

✓ Ensure that your first draft letter or announcement is written by, or in collaboration with, a member of the workshop planning group who has **a stake in the event** and is in tune with the backgrounds and orientations of potential participants. A client comments:

> "*A lot of our workshops are with mechanical engineers in the military. Over the years we have discovered that they want an invitation or announcement that is stripped down to the basics and in point form wherever possible. Clarity of purpose and outcomes is their top priority. Forget trying to soft pedal on issues. Anything other than the essentials is considered flaky by members of this group.*"

✓ If you are working with a **specific sector** (e.g., private, public, environment, health, defence), explore their values and customize the invitation or announcement to reflect those values.

> *In the interests of preserving trees and supporting a future healthy environment, we will be communicating with you from now on by email.*

What to Include in Letters and Announcements

If a workshop is internal to local company employees and takes place on site in a short time-frame as the result of a decision made by senior management, then the invitation will likely be fairly brief and not require information about transportation or cost. The tone will need to convey the urgency of the session and be clear about benefits to employees, customers and shareholders, as well as implementation strategies.

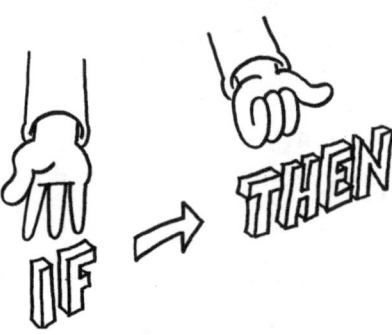

If the workshop is an international think tank on access to clean water in developing countries, then the invitation should include clear instructions about visa requirements, travel arrangements, health insurance, accommodation and expense claims. As well, the invitation can include the selection of participants, how the workshop report will be used, how to acquire an official letter of invitation, etc.

Use the Workshop Diagnostic Framework (Chapter 2) to clarify how you can jazz up your invitation with respect to PIE:

- Will people be enticed by a description of the best scenario emerging from the session?
- Will potential participants be drawn in by a description of the keynote speakers?
- Would a picture of the workshop setting draw readers' attention?
- Would potential participants be intrigued by immediate changes that will happen as a result of decisions made at a session?

Tool 5.1
Letters and Announcements: A Checklist

Review the following list and circle the items you want to include in your invitation. On the right hand side of the list, circle which portion(s) of the PIE (Persuade/Inform/Engage) each item will address.

Agenda

1. Agenda overview, including starting and finishing times and free time for participants, main parts of the agenda and how they flow together   P I E

Background

2. Why this event now: history leading up to the initiative   P I E

3. Pertinent quotations, statistics, articles, related references   P I E

4. How the workshop is aligned with the values of the sponsoring organization or related sector   P I E

5. Signature of person with authority and responsibility; names and credentials of planning committee members   P I E

Cost

6. Cost, e.g., registration, travel, accommodation, reading materials and who is paying   P I E

7. Expense claim   P I E

Logistics and Location

8. Attractions of workshop site, e.g., potential free-time activities   P I E

9. List of important dates leading up to the event, e.g., when registration is due, when questionnaires should be returned   P I E

10. Information about programs for guests   P I E

11. Privacy policy: which of the participants' coordinates you want permission to publish   P I E

12. Confidentiality: who will see your responses to surveys and telephone interviews and how your responses will be used P I E

13. How to register and who to contact for further information P I E

14. Early registration benefits, e.g., reduced costs, free cultural trip P I E

15. Cancellation policy P I E

16. Arrangements for travel and accommodation P I E

17. Predicted weather during the workshop P I E

18. Appropriate clothing for various events P I E

19. Liability issues P I E

Outcomes

20. Purpose, objectives and expected outcomes P I E

21. Secondary benefits, e.g., to a professional field, colleagues, families, organizations, jurisdictions, countries, the globe P I E

22. Reports or proceedings: how prepared, what they include, when published, cost P I E

Participants

23. How participants are being invited, e.g., open to all, invitational to specific groups, mandatory for all P I E

24. How participants can contribute to the purpose P I E

25. Special incentives to attend, e.g., scholarships or reduced registration fees for specific groups P I E

26. Possible objections to participation and how this session will address these P I E

27. A second, closing enthusiastic pitch about benefits of participation, e.g., specific outcomes related to implementation. P I E

Review the circled PIE items on the right hand side of the checklist. Do the portions of your PIE indicate a need to make any changes?

Tool 5.2
Sample First Paragraphs

Sometimes it helps to have a few examples of initial paragraphs for invitations. Each of the following samples conveys a tone that is customized to recipients, based on a PIE formula.

Regional consultation on a draft manual, following a verbal invitation by phone

> *On behalf of the Romanian Working Group on Childhood Hearing (RWGCH), I am delighted to invite you to participate in a regional consultation on a preliminary draft of the RWGCH resource on Early Hearing Detection in Children in Romania. As our planning group chair mentioned in her earlier phone conversation with you, we need your input to ensure that this resource is tailored to meet the needs of professionals in this field.*

Open announcement for a state government marketing workshop

Hey!!!

Do you find it a challenge to get the attention of potential customers?

Do you get frustrated by the lack of response to your ads?

Join other challenged and frustrated marketing types

May 8 - 10

in sunny South Carolina

and get rid of those challenges and frustrations for good.

In-house team-development session

Dear (name)

On behalf of the _____ Alliance of Canada, we thank you for your interest in the Alliance and for your support of the upcoming consultation. In follow-up to your discussion with _____ this letter sets out the purpose and scope of the provincial consultations and survey. Please complete and return the survey to the _____ Secretariat by _____.

As discussed, the Alliance will be hosting a meeting on November 17 and 18 to which small teams of stakeholders from each province and territory will be invited. The purpose of the meeting is to provide an opportunity for stakeholders to collect and share information in an effort to derive what is needed at a national level to support provincial and local work. A key outcome of the meeting will be a shared understanding of the scope of current activity across the country. To be successful, much of this information needs to be collected and shared prior to the November meeting.

Annual conference on affordable housing

The International Affordable Housing Society (IAHS) is an organization involved in policy development in engineering and its associated technologies related to long lasting, socially supportive and affordable housing. The mandate of the IAHS includes disseminating scientific and educational information, and maintaining high standards of ethics. For more than 25 years, the IAHS has been the most prominent world-wide forum for exchange and promotion of research in affordable housing, as epitomized by the Annual Conference convened each January.

On the verge of the third millenium, the Program Chairs (insert names) have prepared an exciting program for the (year) Annual Conference, creating a balance between fundamental research in 'state of the art' presentations during plenary sessions and strategy development during two evening forums. In addition to the Main Program of the Annual Conference, a Satellite Symposium organized by the Local Organizing Committee and Pre-Conference Workshops organized by members of the IAHS have become a regular feature in the last few years – both with attractive programs on specific topics.

The Board of Governors of the IAHS heartily invites you to participate in the Annual Conference, its Satellite Symposium and Workshops, and last but not least to enjoy the warm and hospitable social program with lots of attractions in the Exhibition and Congress Centre and the city of Warsaw, Poland.

Tool 5.3
Soliciting Feedback on a Draft Invitation

To: Planning Committee Members

From:

Re: Workshop Invitation: please review the attached workshop invitation by circling numbers on the checklist below and send your feedback to me by (date).

To what extent does this invitation fit the following criteria:

		Poor			Excellent
a.	Matches the tone of the session, e.g., has just the right degree of formality, informality.	1	2	3	4
b.	Uses an easy-to-read font.	1	2	3	4
c.	Provides an easy-to-understand message at the right language level for potential participants.	1	2	3	4
d.	Describes the workshop as a solution to a problem.	1	2	3	4
e.	Represents fairly the decisions made in the diagnostic framework.	1	2	3	4
f.	Includes all the information required for a favourable response.	1	2	3	4
g.	Suggests easy mechanisms for responding, e.g., email, Web link, fax number, free long distance phone number.	1	2	3	4
h.	Clearly articulates benefits to participants and their affiliated organizations.	1	2	3	4
i.	Provides motivation to register immediately.	1	2	3	4
j.	Has the right balance of "persuade, inform and engage."	1	2	3	4
k.	Has a strong opening and closing.	1	2	3	4

Suggested improvements: _____

_____

_____

Tool 5.4
Invitation to a Network Planning Retreat

To: North County Cardiovascular Network

From: Chair, NCCN Steering Committee

Date:

Re: NCCN Planning Retreat

> *Cardiovascular disease (CVD) is the leading cause of morbidity and mortality in Canada. CVD is also largely preventable both through prevention of the development of CV risk factors and through comprehensive treatment of risk factors in those who develop them.* (NCCN Feasibility Study)

On behalf of the North County Cardiovascular Network (NCCN) Steering Committee, we are delighted to invite you to a Planning Retreat to be held at the University of the North on (date). The purpose of this retreat is to develop a NCCN strategic plan, including purpose, mandate, vision, guiding principles, goals and action steps. The NCCN was initiated as a result of the recently developed National Strategy for Hypertension Prevention and Control and now needs to develop its own plan in alignment with this strategy.

This NCCN Planning event has two main parts:

- Part I is a Public Seminar involving presentations by, and discussions with, keynote speakers in CVD prevention and control. This seminar takes place on (date) at the (location).
- Part II is an Invitational Planning Retreat for community members and will be held at the (location).

We are anticipating attendance at the Planning Retreat to be 40 - 45 community representatives who have a commitment to reducing CVD in the North County area and who want to collaborate with other key people in making a difference in our community's health.

We hope you will accept our invitation to participate in this important event. Your input is needed to ensure that the NCCN is a dynamic and effective health resource in our community. A preliminary agenda is attached to help you plan for this retreat. In the interests of objectivity and efficiency, the workshop process will be managed by an outside facilitator. Further background information will be sent to you following your acceptance.

Please respond to this invitation by contacting the Chair by email at (email address) or by phoning (name) at (number).

Last and Certainly Not Least!

Our network was voted "Best Communicator" at last year's International Congress of Cardiovascular Networks meeting held in Stockholm. We need your input at this planning session to help us maintain this standing over the next three years, as this will ensure our participation at the next International Congress to be held in Tahiti during winter school break.

Yours in health,

(Name)

on behalf of the NCCN Steering Committee:
(Committee member names)

TEMPLATE 5.5
EMAIL ANNOUNCEMENT AND QUESTIONNAIRE FOR AN IN-HOUSE TRAINING WORKSHOP

To:	Staff, Human Resources Department

Re:	Professional Development Workshop on (date): Agenda and Needs Assessment

Date:

From:	Director, Human Resources

It seems appropriate that we are having a professional development workshop on (date) – at the start of a new year of working together.

The purpose of this session is to enhance facilitation skills both internal to our Department and externally with clients. A preliminary agenda is attached for your information.

Our workshop leader is (name), a partner in (company), a very successful local consulting firm. (Name) has been a facilitator for 28 years and has worked extensively in human resources in areas such as recruitment, corporate orientation strategies and executive coaching.

To assist (name) in preparing for this workshop, please respond to the questions below and send your response by email to (address) or fax (number) by (date). (Name) will synthesize your responses into an anonymous report to help us develop the agenda further. Feedback on the results will also be presented in an anonymous form at the workshop.

If you have any questions about the session, please get in touch with (name) by email at the address above.

We are looking forward to spending some time together on our professional development – this session promises to be a stimulating and very practical learning experience in an area where we are continually looking for new ideas.

Regards,

Director, Human Resources

TEMPLATE 5.6
INVITATION TO PARTICIPATE IN A PRE-RETREAT SURVEY

To: Members, East West Engineering Society

From: President, East West Engineering Society

Date:

Re: East West Engineering Society Strategic Planning Survey

The East West Engineering Society (EWES) has identified the revision of its 1990 Strategic Plan as a major project for this year. Many changes have occurred within EWES since 1990 and many of the objectives identified in the previous plan have been realized. Consequently, it is important to articulate future directions that will move the Society into the new millennium.

Outcomes of this planning process will include:
- agreement on a mission statement, core values and a five-year vision for the Society
- agreement on strategic directions and goals for the Society that will enable members to achieve their vision
- enhanced participation in and ownership for the strategic plan and for issues affecting the Society.

The planning process has been structured into five phases:
1. Project Initiation and Liaison
2. Council and Key Stakeholder Consultation, Environmental Scan
3. Member Survey
4. Retreat and Strategic Plan
5. Implementation and Consultation with Members.

To date we have completed Phases 1 and 2 and are now asking for input from members in the form of the attached survey. The purpose of this survey is to gather EWES members' views in three areas relevant to developing a Strategic Plan. All members completing the survey will be involved in a two-day strategic planning workshop in six months' time.

Please complete the survey by going to the following secure Web site address: (address). If you prefer to reply by email or snail mail, you can return your responses to (name of the consulting group on this project) by email: (address) or by mail: (mailing address) by the end of this month. The results will be used, along with other input, as a basis for the EWES Strategic Planning Retreat.

Thank you very much for taking the time to respond to this survey.

Template 5.7
Invitation Requesting Participation in a Mandatory Workshop and Survey

To:	Licensees, Atomic Energy Control Board of Cold County
From:	Director of Licencees (name)
Date:	
Re:	Licensee Survey

The new Nuclear Safety Management Act (NSMA) and the Regional Nuclear Safety Commission Regulations (RNSCR) will come into effect in November of this year. This event will mark the beginning of a new regulatory framework for licensees and create a need for information related to the nature of these new regulations and their implications for all of us.

Many thanks to the following experienced licensees in our region who contributed significant time and effort in the development of these new regulations:

- (list names)

One recommendation made by these licensees was to hold a short series of workshops that supported regional employees in understanding and applying the NSMA and RNSCR.

To this end, the Atomic Energy Authority of Cold County (AEACC) is holding a series of three mandatory workshops for all licencees this year. The purpose of these sessions is to convey expectations outlined in the NSMA and related RNSCR and to enable and promote a smooth transition to compliance with these changes.

These workshops will be held in (location), the regional capital on (dates). We have developed a questionnaire as an important aspect of our preparation for these sessions. The purpose of this document is to gather licensees' perspectives on how the AEACC can address licensees' information needs with respect to the new regulations, i.e.,

> (i) which methods are the most efficient and effective for communicating information, and
>
> (ii) which formats are the most appropriate from a licensee's perspective.

Your input is essential to helping us respond effectively to your information needs. Please complete this confidential questionnaire on the Web by clicking on (address) and following the identified links to the secured site.

Please be candid – your responses are confidential to (name), the consulting company we are working with on this project. We need open, thoughtful and constructive responses to ensure a solid information base for this implementation process. (Name) will be synthesizing your responses into an anonymous report for review by members of the AEACC Implementation Planning Group. Space is provided for your name and phone number so that (name) can contact you if he requires additional information.

Please call (name) at our office (number) within the next two weeks to confirm your participation.

Many thanks for all your support and insights as we move forward through this transition period together. I'm looking forward to working out the next steps together so that we can continue to provide safe, uninterrupted high-quality service to our constituents.

Best regards,

(name)

Director of Licensees

Template 5.8
Advance Announcement: Open Invitation

The Transportation Planning Unit at the University of ABCD is pleased to host the Second Annual Municipal Transportation Congress in (location) from (date). The theme for this Congress is:

Municipal Transportation – Research into Action:
The Public Policy Challenge

The workshop will focus on the importance of targeted research and applications related to efficient and healthy public transport. Inter-city comparisons will be highlighted, including expert presentations from other municipalities.

I personally look forward to your registration and participation at this important annual workshop. Available space and resources require us to limit registration to 60 participants. Register now to avoid disappointment.

I hope to see you in (location) on (date).

Name and Position

Congress Chair

Template 5.9
Written Announcement: Regional Workshop

Central India Information

Regional Business and Economic Writing Workshop

Central India Information (CII) will hold a two-week regional workshop on plain language in business and economic writing in (location) on (date).

This workshop will be open to journalists from the (name) region and CII will pay all expenses. Applicants working on the business desks of their papers will be given preference. Those on the general desk must have a minimum of two years working experience.

As CII is an equal opportunity trainer, we are also giving preference to qualified women journalists interested in business reporting. All applicants must, however, submit two unpublished stories of at least five hundred words to CII.

Applications should reach CII by (date) to enable us to make travel arrangements on time. Those interested should apply to:

The training editor: CII

Fax: (number)   Email: (address)

Central India Information
(address)
(email)

Template 5.10

Short Form Advance Electronic Announcement for a National Conference

Advance Announcement

Meeting the Health Challenge of Prion Diseases

is an upcoming, exciting international research conference

to be held in

(Location)

(Date)

Day One is a symposium featuring presentations and discussions by international authorities on various aspects of prions and prion diseases.

Day Two is a consultation focused on enhancing global research opportunities and results related to prions and prion diseases.

Conference participants will include clinicians, researchers and decision-makers who are interested in a comprehensive and current source of information on prion diseases and an opportunity to provide input to the Global Institutes of Health Research (GIHR) on key global research themes and Requests for Applications (RFA) for the next five to ten years.

This advance announcement closes on (date), after which a general announcement will be made on the GIHR Web site.

Space is limited –

Please register early to avoid disappointment.

Sponsored by (names)

For more information, please go to our Web site at

(address)

and follow the links to the GIHR meeting announcement. (see next page)

TEMPLATE 5.11
LONG FORM ELECTRONIC ANNOUNCEMENT FOR A NATIONAL CONFERENCE

To:

From: Chair, Prions Conference Planning Committee

Date:

Re: International Research Conference: (Date)
Meeting the Health Challenge of Prion Diseases

Prions and prion diseases now constitute major threats to the medical, economic and political well-being of populations around the world. Human prion diseases are uniformly fatal and may be transmitted through a variety of methods such as contaminated blood and blood products, cadaveric pituitary hormones, dura matter implants, corneal transplantation, contaminated neurosurgical instruments and contaminated food sources such as beef. Some prion diseases, such as a variant of Creutzfeldt-Jakob disease (vCJD) are predicted to have potential epidemic impacts on public health.

On behalf of the Conference Organizing Committee, we are pleased to announce this two-day event focused on education and research related to prions and prion diseases. The first day is an educational symposium featuring presentations and discussions by international authorities on various aspects of prions and prion diseases. The report produced on the symposium will provide an expert summary of state-of-the-art knowledge on relevant current issues regarding prions and prion diseases, with a special emphasis on current public health concerns of novel epidemic prion strains.

The second day is a consultation focused on enhancing global research opportunities and results related to prions and prion diseases. Objectives are to:

- summarize key learnings and implications of the symposium for future global research
- identify unique potential research contributions of global scientists and opportunities for international research collaborations
- develop recommendations on priority themes for global research over the next ten years and potential requests for applications (RFA)
- identify opportunities to build capacity through supportive infrastructures
- enhance linkages and interactions among participants, e.g., federal and academic researchers and policy-makers.

This consultation is an initial step in a longer term approach to enhancing opportunities for global research on prions and prion diseases.

This conference is jointly sponsored by (organizations).

Participants

Conference participants will include 125 clinicians, researchers and decision makers from around the world who are interested in a) a comprehensive and current source of information on prions and prion diseases, and b) an opportunity to help shape a global research agenda for this area.

Agenda

This conference will be held at the (hotel) in the (room) in (location) on (date and time). Click here (Web address) for a preliminary agenda.

Registration

If you are interested in attending this conference, please complete the registration form (click here) on this site and return by (date) to the address indicated on the form. Venue capacity is limited to 125 participants: please register early to avoid disappointment.

Background Information

A background information package will be provided closer to the conference. This package will include an udpated conference agenda, a brief history and overview of prion research around the world, fact sheets, biographies of conference speakers, a glossary, and questions to consider prior to the conference.

We are anticipating that this conference will provide insightful learning opportunities and dynamic discussions related to the future of prion diseases and prion related research around the world. We hope you can join us.

Chair, Prions Conference Planning Committee
On behalf of the Conference Organizing Committee:

(Names and positions)

Note: *Venue capacity is limited. Please send in your registration form as soon as possible. Registration closes on (date).*

B. International Requirements

Some participants require an official invitation or letter of support to enable their participation at a workshop.

Official invitations and letters of support are usually provided for individuals requiring a visa for travel to a foreign country. They are issued to convince travel authorities, workplace supervisors or consular officials that a workshop is official business for those attending, e.g., academics, business people, scientists, organizational representatives. Many organizations ask people to apply for an official invitation or letter of support by supplying their co-ordinates and other relevant data.

TIPS

- ✓ Keep in mind that not all countries require invitations or letters of support for visa applications. Check the regulations for all countries involved.

- ✓ Ensure that official invitations and letters of support are only issued to people of appropriate standing, whose credentials and bona fide registration are checked by the workshop organizing committee.

- ✓ Some authorities may object to letters of support which are sent too far in advance of the meeting, e.g., more than four to six months prior to the meeting.

- ✓ Some countries, organizations or governments may require special wording in the invitation so that they conform with local regulations. Be sure to ask for this information in the request form.

- ✓ Be explicit in your workshop information about requirements for official invitations or letters of support, e.g.,

    It is advised that registered delegates to this workshop provide their confirmation of registration to expedite visa applications for entry into our country. The Workshop Organizing Committee will be pleased to send official invitations or letters of support to any delegate making such a request.

    It is understood that such an invitation is intended to help potential attendees raise travel and registration fee funds. It is not a commitment on the part of the Workshop Organizing Committee to provide financial support of any type.

✓ Contact your government regarding letters of support for workshop guests coming to your country. Some countries' requirements are very strict, with the host required to accept full responsibility for the invited person, and to register the invitation with the country's police force. In many situations, workshop sponsors are not comfortable providing such comprehensive guarantees for workshop participants.

> *We cannot issue complete guarantees for any visitors to our workshop. Exceptions are cases where we have personal knowledge of the invited party and a formal letter of recommendation from an acknowledged academic institution. Letters by email cannot be accepted as formal letters. It might be possible to apply directly to our embassy in your country.*

Template 5.12
Request for Official Invitation

To obtain an official invitation, each workshop participant must fill in the following form and send it to the Workshop Secretariat at the following address before (date).

It is the participant's responsibility to submit the invitation to appropriate authorities such as a workplace supervisor or relevant embassy for a visa. We (organization) cannot be held responsible for submission of official letters of invitation or any changes made to the format of the issued letter.

This letter does not pertain to or include a waiver of registration fees or any financial reimbursement.

Requests for letters of invitation will not be honoured after (date).

First Name: _____

Last Name: _____

Organization: _____

Title/Position: _____

Address: _____

Province/State/Region: _____

Postal Code/Zip: _____

Country: _____

Telephone(s): _____

Fax: _____

Email: _____

Reason for attending this event: _____

Please indicate below any special wording required in the Letter of Invitation to ensure that it conforms with your local regulations:

_____

_____

Invitation letters will be sent by fax and Air Mail only. Please indicate your preference by checking one of the following:

Fax: _____   Air Mail: _____

TEMPLATE 5.13

OFFICIAL INVITATION

This letter reflects your personal invitation to visit (location) for a period of one week beginning on or about (date). This visit will provide an opportunity for you to contribute your expertise to a workshop focused on your country's research project on (subject workshop).

Regarding support for your trip, we will provide you with workspace and other work-related support as needed. In addition, we will pay ground and air travel expenses, including one economy class airfare and hotel accommodation for one week. An honorarium of ($) is being provided and paid for through an unrestricted private sector grant.

We understand that you will arrange funding for the remainder of your expenses. If you have any questions about the visit, please contact (name of administrator) at (phone) or by email (address).

> *We are informed that a B1 Business visa is the most appropriate classification for your visit here. In that respect, please take the enclosed Support Letter, along with your valid passport, to the nearest (country) Consulate and request a visa stamp for entry.*

> OR

> *We are informed that your current visa status is appropriate for your visit to (workshop and location). Please make sure to obtain written authorization from your sponsoring institution before coming to (location).*

Our government requires you to maintain medical coverage as well as medical evacuation and repatriation insurance for the duration of your visit. Information on the type of medical coverage required will be sent to you along with the visa application form. You will have the choice of either bringing your own health plan with you, or purchasing one here upon your arrival. If you choose to bring your own health plan, please make sure that the letter from your insurance company is in English or accompanied by an English translation.

If you have questions about visa requirements, please do not hesitate to contact (name and coordinates). Any questions regarding your visa application should be addressed to (name and coordinates).

We are most enthusiastic about having you participate in this important session. Your experience and expertise are highly respected and would be a significant benefit for the 50 researchers in this field whom we are inviting from around the globe.

We are looking forward to your reply.

Enclosures: Support Letter to (Embassy, Consulate or Immigration Office)

Template 5.14
Letter of Support

The above-named individual has been invited by (workshop sponsor) to come to a workshop on (title) for the period of one week, (date to date). His/her host at the workshop is (name and title).

This workshop has been held annually for the past 15 years and is a prestigious event which scientists in this field all over the world look forward to attending. Participants include 50 of the top scientists in the area of (describe).

The purpose of this workshop is to ...

Objectives are to ...

This workshop is timely given current discussions at the United Nations regarding the crisis in (name area). Participants at this event will have an opportunity to work in multi-sector partnerships to address this issue at a global level. Additional benefits to the countries represented at this workshop include ...

The workshop is being sponsored by (stakeholders) represented on the workshop secretariat. We will be providing (name) with workspace and other work-related support as needed. In addition, we will pay ground and air travel expenses including one economy class airfare and hotel accommodation for one week. (Name) will not receive a salary nor will he be employed by (sponsor) during his stay. An honorarium of ($) is being provided and paid for through an unrestricted private sector sponsor.

We are informed that a B1 Business visa is the most appropriate classification for this visit. Therefore we respectfully request that you use this Letter of Support, along with a valid passport, as substantiation for a visa stamp for entry to (country).

If you require additional information, please do not hesitate to contact me at the workshop secretariat by fax at (number), phone at (number) or email at (address).

We are grateful for all due courtesy extended to (name) by your personnel.

Thank you.

Signature

C. Challenging Situations

A well constructed invitation or announcement is customized to fit the workshop environment: it has the right tone, approach and wording to appeal to participants and to set an appropriate workshop climate.

Some workshops exist in challenging environments. The environment of a workshop can be the organizational history, the small "p" and big "P" politics, the backgrounds and perspectives of participants, the expected impact of the workshop on participants and their organizations, and the anxieties that participants may have about the agenda or process. When invitations and announcements take environment into consideration, they are customized to address the perspectives of participants in relation to the workshop objectives.

Before the invitations have gone out, facilitators/managers are often aware of environmental challenges they will need to address, e.g., people who want to come for a few hours of a one-day workshop; organizations that want to send three or four representatives when there is only space for one; people who will want media in attendance when the client thinks it is inappropriate.

By addressing these challenges in your workshop invitation, you can help prevent them from becoming on-site problems.

Tool 5.15
Paragraphs for Challenging Situations

Challenge: Boundaries on discussion

Sample paragraph from the representative of a Board Executive Committee for a public policy workshop where you want clear boundaries on discussion:

> *Your Board Executive Committee has assigned the highest possible priority to addressing the widespread shortages in human resources related to cancer care, focusing first on the core disciplines of Radiation and Medical Oncology in cancer treatment centres across the country. Issues for disciplines other than in radiotherapy and systemic treatment services will be the subject of further study during a second stage of this project. They are not on the agenda for this workshop.*

Challenge: Exclusion of media

Sample paragraph from the Chair, Board of Governors, of a multi-national accounting firm, regarding the exclusion of media from a high-profile roundtable on ethics:

> *We have received several inquiries about the possibility of including the media at this roundtable. Given that this is our initial session on this topic and that we want to entertain a variety of wide-ranging perspectives in our discussions, your Board of Governors has decided not to invite media participation at this time. There will be future opportunities for the media to be present at sessions when our approach and policy are at a more mature stage of development.*

Challenge: Mandatory participation

Workshop participants in XYZ industry are notorious for part-time participation in sessions. The challenge is to create an invitation that is unequivocal about attendance and participation.

Sample paragraphs from a person with authority and influence in relation to participants:

> *This planning workshop will require your full participation. Please plan to attend all sessions as described in the attached agenda. If you are unable to attend any part of the workshop due to previous commitments, please contact your immediate supervisor who has been made aware of the importance of your contributions during these discussions.*

OR

> *This planning workshop will require your full participation. Please plan to attend all sessions as described in the attached agenda. If you are unable to attend any part of the workshop, please contact us so that we can arrange for someone else with your background and experience to participate.*

Challenge: Participation in a series of Think Tanks

Sample paragraph from the Director of Human Resources to encourage full participation in a series of workshops:

> *On (date) our corporate group will be having its second Think Tank. The first Think Tank took place in (location) on (date) where the initial work was done on the future of our Nutriceuticals Division. This served as the basis for the development of a new organizational structure which led to the first formal meeting of the Board of Directors in (location) on (date).*
>
> *The purpose of this Think Tank is to continue with and build on this work. To be successful we need everyone in our division to participate wholeheartedly.*

Challenge: Participation without prejudice

Sample paragraph from the Chief Executive Officer of Global Environment Group to encourage Executive Directors of Non-Government Organizations to participate in a forum without being committed to outcomes, but with a commitment to explore (with their Boards of Directors) ways to act on the results of the workshop:

> *Participants in this Partnership Forum represent 23 non-government environmental organizations that:*
> - *are national in scope*
> - *have an explicit mandate for research related to wildlife management, and*
> - *have the capacity and commitment to initiate and implement research partnerships.*
>
> *Forum participants represent a variety of perspectives and will be participating without prejudice, i.e., it is expected that they will consult further with their organizations before making any commitment to partner with the Global Environment Group or other organizations at the Forum on ways to implement recommendations developed at the Forum.*

Challenge: Persuasion to collaborate

Sample paragraphs in a letter from a responsible senior public servant to employees in a large Department:

> *The Clerk of the Privy Council and his three Deputy Minister Committees have recently reported on three key issues that must be addressed to build a highly skilled public service:*
> - *Recruitment: replenishing the public service with the "best and the brightest"*
> - *Retention: creating a workplace and a culture that will retain our new and existing workforce, and*
> - *Learning: building the federal public service into a learning organization.*
>
> *Many very positive recommendations have been made and our office is now assigned the task of bringing together all of these suggestions into a master strategy that creates a vibrant public service for the future. We need to do this together in the best spirit of public service collaboration.*

Challenge: Restricted participation

Sample paragraph from an organizing committee chair regarding restricted participation in a workshop that a large number of people want to attend:

> *Given cost restrictions we are limiting this initial meeting to one representative per affiliate organization. Once the second stage of this project has been funded we will be implementing a more comprehensive consultation with broader participation.*

Challenge: Special financial support

Sample paragraph announcing scholarships for young researchers:

> *Scholarships Available for Young Researchers*
>
> *The future of research in this area lies in building our country's research capacity. If you are a young researcher who fulfills the criteria listed below, please complete the attached scholarship application to attend this two-day international conference, all expenses paid. Ten scholarships will be awarded by the conference planning committee.*

Challenge: Suggest participants

A workshop on family impact issues is being held at the local level, with invitations restricted to government policy-makers involved in the area. The following paragraph is in a letter inviting government personnel to suggest participants who are active in this area in their municipalities.

Sample paragraphs in a letter from a workshop planning committee member:

> *The Family Impact Seminar is designed to provide local policy-makers with objective, nonpartisan information on current family issues. The goal is to encourage policy-makers to recognize the impact of policies on families, and to encourage the assessment of family impacts by persons who develop and implement policy.*
>
> *A local policy-maker is a person who:*
> - *makes decisions regarding public or private policy (helps design or develop laws, rules, codes, etc., that will affect the community and families)*
> - *sets workplace policies that affect employees*
> - *helps decide how policies will be implemented*
> - *is influential in shaping policy that affects local citizens.*
>
> *Sample categories (alphabetical order) of local policy-makers include:*
>
> | | |
> |---|---|
> | *Business/Industry/Labor* | *City Council* |
> | *City Mayor* | *County Board* |
> | *County Executive* | *Hospital Board* |
> | *Housing Authority* | *Judiciary* |
> | *Law Enforcement* | *Non-profit Organization* |
> | *Religious Leaders* | *School Administration* |
> | *School Boards* | *Social and Human Services* |
> | *Town Boards* | *Village Boards* |
> | *Zoning Boards* | |
>
> *Please nominate one individual from each category to participate in this workshop and we will send them a formal invitation.*

Challenge: Preventing part-time participation

Participants entering and leaving a workshop at unscheduled times can have an impact on sessions in a number of ways, depending on the workshop purpose and objectives.

If a workshop is open to all, is focused on individual learning, and there are no group discussions or learning tasks, then the impact can be minimal. However, in many invitational sessions, the number and makeup of individuals in plenary are developed through criteria designed to support discussion and decision making. In these situations, if participants are present for some discussions and absent for others then their points of view are not included in an organized and focused way throughout the discussions and this affects the quality of discussion and decision making.

In most invitational sessions, people coming in late miss out on essential climate-setting activities during the first part of the workshop. This is where people meet one another; learn essential information in relation to their participation; agree on key terms; and generally come together as a group by setting norms and negotiating how they want to relate to one another so that they will function well together as a group.

Part-time participation also adds an additional burden for facilitators. If people are entering and leaving a workshop, the facilitator needs to find a way to acknowledge these exits and entrances without calling too much attention to them. Humour may have an initially positive impact but will only go so far. Workshop participants usually notice when their numbers are changing and want to know why people left and who the new people are.

Finally, clients who pay for participants to come to a workshop, e.g., to develop a national strategy or to do issues analysis, often pay travel and accommodation costs and occasionally an honorarium to support participants' attendance. This financial support often brings with it an unstated obligation to attend and participate fully in workshop activities. Participants need to understand this informal contract.

Sample paragraph from an organizing committee inviting board members to develop a strategic plan for their non-government organization:

> *Given the importance of everyone's presence for discussions, we have scheduled the workshop to accommodate travel times from coast to coast to coast. Please make your travel arrangements through our conference office: (Name) will ensure that all flights enable everyone to participate in the entire session and still arrive home in time for dinner.*

Challenge: Urgency and commitment

Sample paragraphs in a letter to employees from the Executive Director of a public art gallery who wants to convey urgency and commitment about accessibility for people with disabilities:

> *Our task in this workshop is to build a living legacy in arts and culture in our community. The way ahead is through fundamental policy changes that will enhance the accessibility of our programs and buildings to all citizens in our community. To do this we need some time away from day-to-day pressures where we can think in new ways about what works and what doesn't in relation to access.*
>
> *I want people to notice a substantial difference in how we do our business. This is not an opportunity to make small adjustments or tweak existing programs. This is an opportunity for large scale change – for becoming more citizen-centred in how we function.*

Chapter 6

Logistics, Locations and Layouts

★★★★★★★★★★★★★★★★★★★★★★★

★★★★★★★★★★★★★★★★★★★★★★★

Logistics, Locations and Layouts

In workshop management, logistics, locations and layouts are about getting the details right – details that sometimes seem small but can have a big impact on the success of a session.

When logistics are working well, you have the supplies you need when you need them. When you have the right workshop location, it supports participants in contributing to a session; they feel comfortable and able to focus on meeting outcomes without being distracted. Details about room layout can also contribute to productivity: putting panel members on a small riser ensures they can be seen; if you can avoid putting chairs directly under heating and air conditioning vents, you will have fewer complaints about room temperature from participants.

This chapter provides tips, tools and templates for three aspects of workshop management:

A. Logistics

B. Locations

C. Layouts.

A systematic approach to organizing logistics, locations and layouts minimizes crisis management and prevents the frustration and lost productivity that accompanies poor organization. And in the event that something unanticipated surprises you, the section in this chapter on logistical letdowns should provide you with some backup strategies.

Part II: Tips, Tools and Templates

A. Logistics

Logistics are unique to each workshop and each facilitator/manager. What is a "must have" item for one session is on an optional list for another. Being ready for all eventualities distinguishes your service as a workshop manager: participants usually miss the "must haves" when they are not there, but often don't notice them when they are.

This section explores six areas for workshop logistics:

1. Session-Specific Logistics
2. Mobile Office Logistics
3. Technical and Audiovisual Logistics
4. Personal Logistics
5. International and Cross-Cultural Logistics
6. Travel Logistics.

Customize the checklists provided to suit specific sessions and your own requirements and approaches.

1. Session-Specific Logistics

Review the Diagnostic Framework (Chapter 2) to identify areas where you can target logistics to specifications, challenges and choices in support of workshop outcomes. Logistics-related sections of the Diagnostic Framework include:

- Purpose and Objectives
- Food
- Roles
- Best scenario
- Date
- Location
- Type of session
- Participant identification.

TIPS

✓ Sometimes the **smallest details** can make people feel comfortable with themselves, one another and the session's environment.

> *It is the explicit job of every facilitator to cultivate a bone-deep feel for the participant: this is how magic is generated. If you believe you're in the business of serving the customer better, then you have to move the centre of gravity of the workshop to where the focus meets the needs of the participants.*[1]

✓ If you have been asked for or needed something **more than once** at different workshops, add it to your logistics checklist.

✓ When using the customized checklist at the end of this section on Logistics, think about how you can **add value** to items so that they optimize participants' experiences at the workshop.

✓ **Customize your checklist** for each workshop. Send a copy to your client, noting items they will need to provide.

✓ Make **food choices** that reflect the purpose of the workshop. Communicate this to participants in their handouts and in the introduction to the session, as in the following examples:

- You will no doubt notice that our lunch today is in keeping with our position as an organization focused on heart health. Food choices are heart healthy and low in cholesterol.

- We're proud of our workshop menu. All of these selections are items that our airline serves to passengers in executive class.

- Because this is the national meeting of the World Poverty Alliance, our lunch menu is meant to demonstrate that with appropriate education people can plan tasty and nutritious meals for less money than expected. Today's lunch cost our organization $1.50 per person and is consistent with our country's food guide. Please take these recipes (found under your plate) home so that you can share them with friends and neighbours.

- Meals at this workshop are designed to accommodate the large number of vegetarian participants. Please let your server know if you would like the vegetarian option.

---

1. LaBarre, Polly. "Leader: Feargal Quinn" in *Fast Company Magazine*. Boston, MA: Fast Company, November 2001, p. 92.

✓ As a **value-add**, look for edible "treats" that can highlight agenda items, spark meaning, images, social connection or fun, e.g., customized fortune cookies in a strategic planning session focused on visioning:

> *"The sayings in the fortune cookies were right on – they helped us to think about the future in concrete ways."*

✓ Protect everyone's **health and safety** with announcements and/or notices:

- One workshop participant is severely allergic to peanuts and bananas. If you have anything with you that includes peanuts or bananas please bring it forward now so that we can place it aside for the end of the day.

- As mentioned in our last communication with you, two workshop participants are allergic to perfume. If you are wearing perfume today please remove as much as possible. Thank you.

✓ Think of **images** that the type of session evokes that can be used to make the session memorable. Incorporate images into handouts, stickers, giveaways such as squeeze balls, pens, etc.

> *"That sponge in the shape of a key still sits on my desk – it fits my hand perfectly and I pick it up and squeeze it frequently. It's a good reminder of the keys to increasing market share that we talked about in that session."*

A Think Tank conjures up images such as a lightbulb; a Search Conference can be associated with flashlights, binoculars, or a magnifying glass. Keep in mind that what's memorable for one group may be considered flaky by another.

✓ Review the **best scenario** described in the Diagnostic Framework (Chapter 2). Think about how your logistics can exceed the identified expectations and add value, e.g., add a giveaway that reinforces an important component of the agenda, such as different coloured pens to distinguish the discussion topics at different table groups.

Name Badges and Place Cards

Personal identification is an important and often overlooked aspect of workshop logistics. There are many **options for what to include** on name badges and place cards:

- first name
- last name
- middle initials
- educational degrees
- affiliations, e.g., organizations, place of employment, name of voluntary committee
- position in a sponsoring organization, e.g., committee chair, board member, work position
- formal title, e.g., job position, military rank, religious level, academic position, institutional ranking. Some people prefer not to have university degrees on name tags; others, such as some physicians and professors are not comfortable unless they are addressed as "Dr." or "Professor." If people will be relating to each other through ideas rather than education or job position, it may be wise to omit degrees or formal titles.

What you include on a name badge or place card is a strategic decision, as it affects the tone of a session and how people will relate to one another. Do you want to encourage an informal tone, with people using first names? If so, make the first name larger on the name badge and don't include educational degrees. For more formal settings, use Mr., Ms., Mrs., Dr., Professor, etc.

✓ Decide whether **name badges, place cards or both are appropriate**, e.g.,
  - If you don't know the people in the session but they know each other, use place cards instead of name badges.
  - If people are shifting groups more than once, name badges will stay with them; place cards may not.

✓ Use a **font type and size** that most people can read easily. A 16 point easy-to-read font on name badges will ensure that names can be seen at a short distance.

✓ What is the **minimum amount of information** that will enable participants to carry on an intelligent conversation? Too much information on name badges makes them difficult to read.

✓ Given the purpose and objectives of the session, what type of name badge will best **support people getting to know one another** with a minimum of interaction, e.g., small, large, more information, less information, etc.?

✓ Ensure that what is on the name badge **supports the type of workshop**. If the session is a roundtable, where everyone's input is valued equally, ensure that name badges and place cards reflect that principle, i.e., first and last name and perhaps geographical location, without degrees, positions or ranks. Additional information can always be provided in a participant list.

The question about whether to include educational degrees or the title of "Dr." often comes up when discussing name badges. In university and professional settings, providing this information may be the norm. Discuss this decision with your client in light of the diagnostic framework so that you make a decision that supports session outcomes.

✓ **Identify roles** that require quick, easy recognition during larger workshops. Table facilitators, planning committee members, local hosts, etc., can be identified in a variety of ways to reflect the session's level of formality, e.g., coloured name badges, dots or coloured ribbon on name badges, arm bands, hats or jackets.

✓ If an objective is networking, enter information on name badges into a **database**, generating a helpful post-workshop resource for participants.

Method to Magic

Diagnostic: You receive a request to facilitate a think tank on accreditation policies for 20 massage therapists from across your state. The planning group decides that a substantial number of documents must be distributed in advance for review by participants. After reading the information, you try to persuade planning group members that executive summaries of these documents would suffice, but to no avail. "We know this group – they like all the details."

Decisions: Provide supplies in an attractive format that will help participants manage and organize large amounts of paper: sticky notes in different shapes, sizes and colours, filing flags, a personalized binder with customized tabs and a think tank logo on the cover; highlighter pens in a variety of colours; hand cream to soothe dry fingers as a result of sorting through papers.

Even though you had a different opinion about the background documents, you understood what we wanted to do and went with our decision efficiently. You even attended to small details that weren't in our contract, like providing hand cream on tables – a particularly thoughtful touch for massage therapists. We really appreciated your high-service attitude – it made everyone feel well accommodated.

Tool 6.1
Checklist: Session-Specific Logistics

Customize the following alphabetical list according to your priorities, e.g., facial tissues may be a high priority for someone with allergies, and a low priority for others.

1. A copy of the final agenda, including break and meal times and special dietary requirements to location staff
2. Binders, file folders, etc., for organizing materials
3. Cultural norms, e.g., dress, tobacco, liquor
4. Directions to the location
5. Expense sheets
6. Extra copies of the pre-workshop package and background materials – three for every ten participants
7. Extra copy of speaker's notes
8. Facial tissues
9. Final detailed session design
10. Garbage cans
11. Giveaways
12. Meetings set up with client and/or planning committee members during and after the session
13. Menu choices and preferences
14. Mints on tables
16. Name badges and extra blanks: two extra blanks for every 12 participants
17. Notice about allergies that could impact participation, e.g., nuts, perfumes, etc.
18. Organizing tools, e.g., sticky note pads – sizes and colours
19. Pens and paper
20. Pitchers or bottles of water within reach of each person in the room
21. Place cards
22. Reading glasses[2]

---

2. Optegos (reading glasses without arms) are available through: www.optego.com.

22. Room set-up

23. Scribe, recording secretary or transcriber

24. Signage at the location

25. Translation of signs, documents

26. Travel arrangements and costs

27. Worksheets (task sheets, process frameworks, evaluations etc.)

28. Value-adds, e.g., prizes, posters, sponge stress balls

29. _____

30. _____

31. _____

32. _____

METHOD TO MAGIC

Diagnostic: You receive a request to facilitate a state planning session on human resource issues in prison facilities. Workshop participants are leaders of various union groups and the session is quite charged politically. Your client is apprehensive about her presentation and how it will be received. You have reviewed your logistics checklists several times and have arranged for on-site assistance to ensure that absolutely nothing is overlooked.

Decisions: About ten minutes before she speaks, your client informs you in an embarrassed tone that her skirt hem thread has unravelled. She is already nervous about the session to start with and this just causes more tension. You stay calm and offer her a choice of scotch tape, duct tape, a stapler or a needle and thread – all are in your workshop kit.

I couldn't believe that such a small thing could upset me so much. I guess it was all the tension at the session that really got on my nerves. Your workshop kit made the difference – once the problem was solved, I could really focus and get on with the day.

2. Mobile Office Logistics

Whether you are travelling to another city for a session or holding it in the same building as your office, it is essential to have your workshop supplies within easy reach. The following tips enable effective on-site management by having a mobile office at your fingertips.

TIPS

✓ **Different types of workshop goals and agendas** require different supplies. Review each section of your agenda and check off items you will require, e.g., coloured dots for vote-based decision making or large sticky notes for brainstorming.

✓ Keep a **plastic box stocked** with your mobile office items so that it's ready to take with you. Keep a customized, plasticized checklist in the box for handy reference.

✓ If you are asked for, or need, **something more than once**, add it to your mobile office checklist.

Tool 6.2
Checklist: Mobile Office Logistics

Circle the number of items that apply.

1. Calculator
2. Company notepad and business cards
3. Day book or electronic scheduler
4. Dots in various sets (4 each, 5 each, 6 each)
5. Elastics
6. Eraser
7. Extra paper
8. Giveaways
9. Glue stick
10. Hand cream
11. Masking tape that doesn't remove paint from walls
12. Paper clips - large and small
13. Pens and pencils: assorted colours
14. Printer paper
15. Post-it flip charts that adhere to walls without removing paint
16. Ruler
17. Scissors
18. Stapler and staples (appropriate sizes)
19. Stick pins for bulletin boards
20. Sticky notepads - 2 sizes and 2 colours
21. Tape (transparent and masking)
22. Three-hole punch
23. Watch with timing feature
24. Water based, easy-to-see, non-permanent, unscented markers
25. White-out liquid for making quick copy changes
26. _____
27. _____

3. Technical and Audiovisual Logistics

Review your Diagnostic Framework (Chapter 2) to decide what technical and audiovisual support is required for a session. Keep in mind that not all sessions benefit from a lot of technology: one flip chart and an overhead projector may be more appropriate in an informal workshop in a community centre than an LCD projector and networked computers. Technology is often not needed in small group situations where you want to encourage disclosure.

On the other hand, if you are facilitating/managing a large trilingual consultation involving 75 scientific experts from around the world in a controversial ethical area, you may need three LCD projectors, one for each official language, three screens, 15 flip charts, eight portable networked computers (one for each small discussion group), a video playback machine, satellite hook-up to off-site conference sessions in other countries, one microphone on each table, a taping system to support report writing, microphones on the head table, a lavalier microphone for the facilitator, three portable microphones for plenary discussions and an electronic key-pad voting system to encourage inclusiveness and record opinions anonymously.

The key to effective technical and audiovisual support is to think strategically, and to make sure that decisions are aligned with conclusions in the Diagnostic Framework.

TIPS

✓ Consider the following **questions** when thinking about technical and audiovisual requirements:

- What kind of ambience do you want to have in the session, e.g., intimate, casual, formal, informal, interactive, and how could you use technical and audiovisual support to achieve that ambience?
- How much experience do participants have with AV equipment?
- How could technical or audiovisual support contribute to your workshop purpose and objectives?
- How could technical or audiovisual support detract from the workshop purpose and objectives?
- How much time or training will be required for participants to become comfortable using technical supports such as computers, software programs?

✓ Provide a **lavalier microphone** for speakers who like to move around while talking. Check or replace the batteries every three hours; have extra batteries on hand. A lavalier microphone leaves your hands free while a portable microphone is hand held.

✓ Caution speakers to make sure their lavalier microphones are turned off when they use **washroom facilities**!

Logistics, Locations and Layouts

METHOD TO MAGIC

Diagnostic: You are facilitating a workshop for 120 senior managers from across your international office products corporation. The featured speaker is bringing his own computer projector system and arrives five minutes before his presentation is scheduled to begin. As you are helping him to set up, he announces he needs an extension cord.

Decisions: You reach for the one in your kit, plug it in and the presentation starts on time. No waiting for hotel staff to arrive.

Thanks for helping me get set up so quickly. I was really nervous after being delayed by that accident on the freeway but your quick response was reassuring. That's quite a bag of supplies you have!

- ✓ Take into account the **personal preferences** of speakers. One president of a multi-national high-tech company doesn't like to use an LCD projector – he prefers to draw on blank overheads.

- ✓ **Test all equipment** one hour before a session starts and then with each speaker to ensure that everything is lined up and ready to go when the start time on your agenda rolls around.

- ✓ Make sure the **microphone system is compatible** if microphones are rented.

- ✓ Ensure that electrical **cords are taped down** so that people don't trip over them. If you have a bulky connection in the middle of a room, put a small table over it to prevent participants from stumbling.

- ✓ Check for dead spaces **where microphones won't work**, or worse, where feedback will occur.

- ✓ What do you need to **ensure** that the equipment you are using will **work well**? For example., extra bulb for projector, clear sightlines, pointer for slides?

- ✓ What **special lighting** is required? Who will attend to lighting requirements during the workshop, e.g., adjust brightness before and after a PowerPoint presentation?

- ✓ Have a **technology back-up strategy** in place. If a PowerPoint presentation doesn't work or your speaker loses her disk, have overheads and a projector available or provide hard copies of the presentation .

✓ Carry a **power bar and extension cord** for use in the workshop room or your hotel room.

✓ Identify the **on-site technical support person.** Keep the name and contact number handy.

✓ Provide clear guidelines on **"tech etiquette."** Ask people to turn off cell phones and pagers or put them on vibrate.

✓ If you want to take **photographs, videotape or record** parts of a session, let participants know beforehand and ask for their permission to proceed. Give people time to talk to you (e.g., during a break) before you start taking pictures.

> *" Thanks so much for letting us know about the group photograph ahead of time. I didn't want to say anything in front of the group, but I can't have my picture appear anywhere at any time. I'm in a police protection program. It's OK to have my name on the participant list because that's been changed. "*

✓ Do you want to **record the meeting**? In some situations, such as when you are preparing a proceedings, recordings can be helpful when doing summaries of presentations. However, when you want people to speak candidly, taping discussions can inhibit disclosure.

✓ When finalizing room set-up, **sit in chairs** in hard-to-see locations to make sure everyone in the room can see screens and speakers.

Tool 6.3
Checklist: Technical and Audiovisual Logistics

Circle the numbers of items that apply.

1. Blackboard or whiteboard
2. Camera and film
3. CD/tape player
4. CDs, videos, tapes
5. Chalk
6. Computer(s), printer(s)
7. Displays
8. Extension cord, three-way plug adaptor
9. Extra batteries for portable computers
10. Extra blank overhead transparencies
11. Extra diskettes, CD-ROMs
12. Extra overhead projector bulbs
13. Flipcharts (stands and paper) – specify number
14. Markers – water-based, easy-to-see, unscented, various colours, new
15. Microphones – cordless, on tables, at the head table – specify number
16. Overhead pens (three sets non-permanent)
17. Podium
18. Pointer (battery-powered) for highlighting items on screens
19. Portable hard drive to store reports and documents created on site
20. Poster displays
21. Post-it flip charts that adhere to walls without removing paint
22. Power bar
23. Projection equipment: overhead, film, video, LCD, data, etc.
24. Resource tables

Part II: Tips, Tools and Templates

25. Riser for speaker table
26. Screen(s)
27. Table or stand for projection equipment
28. Three-prong adaptor
29. Videos and DVDs: blank and filled
30. Videocamera and film
31. Video monitor, television
32. _____
33. _____
34. _____

4. Personal Logistics

What does it take for you to feel comfortable and confident in your workshop setting? Whatever those items are, they go in your personal logistics kit.

TIPS

✓ Think about how you react to stressful situations and bring along **whatever you need to cope**, e.g., a heating pad, a cold pack, a mystery novel, a pair of slippers, medication for headaches or a sore back, a yoga mat, cold-sore cream, an extra pair of comfortable shoes.

✓ Take care of your feet. Bring whatever you need to be **comfortable** standing and walking for long periods of time.

✓ If you wear **contact lenses**, ensure you have comfort drops and an extra pair of lenses in your kit.

Tool 6.4
Checklist: Personal Logistics Kit

Circle the numbers of items that apply.

1. Alarm clock
2. Books, magazines for relaxed reading
3. Business cards
4. Cell phone, hand held accessories
5. Clothes for local weather conditions
6. Exercise gear, walking shoes, bathing suit
7. Eyewear: glasses, contact lenses and cleaning equipment, comfort drops, sunglasses
8. Facial tissues
9. Favourite music and player
10. Healthy, energizing snacks
11. Hotel comfort kit: slip-on footwear, moisturizers, lounging pyjamas, humidifier
12. Internet hook-up cords
13. Lip balm
14. Makeup
15. Medicine
16. Pictures of loved ones
17. Shampoo and conditioner
18. Short-wave radio
19. Sunscreen
20. Throat lozenges
21. Vitamin supplements
22. Water
23. Water purifier
24. Watch that is easy to read
25. _____
26. _____

5. International and Cross-Cultural Logistics

Multilingual and/or multicultural situations provide special challenges related to logistics. What is normal and acceptable in one culture may not be appropriate in another.

TIPS

✓   Ask the client to designate **official workshop languages**. In countries such as Canada and Switzerland where there is more than one official language, enquire about policies and legal requirements[3] related to language so that you can follow through with respect to how the workshop functions.

✓   Enable people speaking different languages to be **comfortable** in sessions.
   - Ensure signage is in all the official languages that will be used during the workshop.
   - Provide signs for one-language tables made up in all the official languages of the workshop. For example, if there are unilingual Spanish, French and English workshop participants, a sign saying that one table is for "French speaking participants only" should be in French, Spanish and English so that all participants can read it.

✓   Depending on where your meeting is being held, explore **organizational and province/state/country policies** regarding culturally specific matters such as dress, tobacco, liquor, feedback and evaluation to ensure that you are familiar with the norms of the people in the workshop. During the opening session for the workshop, explain these norms clearly so that people are aware of how their behaviour will affect and be interpreted by others in the workshop, e.g.:

   > *This workshop is being held in a specially designated hotel in this city where foreign dress is permitted. Women may dress as they choose in this area as long as their arms and legs are completely covered. Please remember that outside of this hotel both women and men must dress in traditional clothing, as indicated in your registration kits. Failure to dress appropriately will result in detainment or immediate expulsion from the country.*

✓   On your registration form, ask participants **which of the official workshop languages** they would prefer to use at the workshop and in which official language they prefer to receive their background documents.

✓   Provide **translators with copies** of the workshop agenda, the pre-workshop package, handouts and other background documents so that they can familiarize themselves with the material being discussed and any technical terms that will need translating.

✓   Ask your destination country for information and brochures about **cultural norms, laws, sensitivities.**

---

3. Canada's Official Languages Act is available at www.tbs-sct.gc.ca/ollo/legislation-lègislation/index_e.asp

Tool 6.5

Checklist: International and Cross-Cultural Logistics

Circle the numbers of items that apply.

Cultural Sensitivities

1. Guidelines for business and workshop etiquette, e.g., simple greetings, handshakes, appropriate dress, how to address senior officials and elders

2. Etiquette related to meals

3. Customs related to gender, e.g., male - female seating arrangements

4. Social expectations of hosts, e.g., meals together

5. _____

6. _____

7. _____

8. _____

Translation

1. Translation services, e.g., simultaneous translation during workshop proceedings

2. Space for translation booth at the back of the room

3. Materials (agendas, handouts, worksheets) to translators ahead of time

4. Whisper translators for use during small group discussions

6. Travel Logistics

Managing sessions on the road creates logistical challenges for everyone: facilitator, manager, participants.

TIPS

✓ **Provide location coordinates** to participants before the workshop so that they can leave them with others at work and home if they need to be reached.

✓ Think about being on the road during **the best of times and the worst of times**. If your schedule turns out to be more flexible than planned, do you have what you need to enjoy yourself during your time off, e.g., a bathing suit, running shoes, a book or magazine? If you end up having the worst workshop of your life, do you have what it takes to relax and calm down, e.g., a contact for a massage, a colleague's phone number, the name of a good restaurant?

✓ Consider creating a **Cost Sharing Travel Formula** where the total estimated travel cost for all participants is divided by the number of participants.

In many countries, meetings and conferences are held in the most central, highly populated locations. As a result, the same people and organizations from less populated areas bear the brunt of the most expensive travel costs. In Canada – given the size of our country – we often use a geography-based cost sharing principle where everyone pays the same amount to get to a meeting regardless of whether they are local or not. This means that someone from Nunavut (northern territory of Canada) pays the same as someone from the city in which the meeting is being held.

✓ Encourage participants from other countries to purchase **health insurance** for the time they are away from home.

Tool 6.6

Checklist: Travel Logistics

Circle the numbers of items that apply.

1. Cash for countries of origin and destination so that you can pay additional airport charges, e.g., security, airport improvements, departure taxes

2. Driver's licence, e.g., for car rentals

3. Financial resources, e.g., traveller's cheques, international currencies, charge cards

4. Information on things to do and places to go during time off at your destination

5. Luggage to fit travel requirements, e.g., size and weight of carry-on luggage, no security-risk items in luggage

6. Map of walking tours and trails

7. One change of clothing in carry-on luggage in case luggage is delayed or lost

8. Out-of-province/state/country health insurance

9. Photo Identification, e.g., Health Card, driver's licence

10. Prescriptions, e.g., to validate medicines in luggage or in case of a required purchase

11. Remedies for possible travel ailments, e.g., anti-diarrhea pills, water purifier

12. Sweater or jacket in carry-on luggage

13. Travel documents, e.g., passport, visa, photocopies of passport and visa carried separately from actual documents

14. Travel first-aid kit, e.g., Band-Aids, needles, antiseptic cream

15. Travel tickets, e.g., air, train, car rental

16. Weather in destination country, e.g., impact on clothing requirements, sun hat, sunscreen

17. _____

18. _____

19. _____

20. _____

Logistical Letdowns

When something happens inadvertently regarding logistics and you have to recover immediately, you have a logistical letdown. Your ability to spring back from a logistical oversight, setback or crisis can be a real test of problem solving skills.

Here are some tips on generating magic from logistical letdowns — or at least surviving them!

TIPS

✓ Decide what is most **appropriate to tell** workshop participants, e.g., if the situation is about to impact on their workshop participation, tell them what is happening; if you can resolve the situation, don't distract participation by informing the group of the dilemma.

> *"At a residential retreat, my heart jumped when I discovered that the 30-minute video that was to be played and discussed at 9 am the next morning had been left at the office. After the evening session, I politely excused myself from the social activities, hopped in my car and drove 45 minutes to recover the video. To this day, no one knows about my midnight rescue mission!"*

✓ If **something important is missing,** ask yourself:[4]

- Can you or someone else get it? Can it be faxed or sent electronically? Can the facility staff or others deliver or courier it?

- Can you replace it? Does facility staff know if it can be rented or bought in the area?

- Can you improvise? What could you do as a substitute?

---

4. Adapted from: Reitz, Helen L. and Marilyn Manning. *The One Stop Guide to Workshops*. New York, New York: Irwin Professional Publishing, 1994, p. 276

✓ What are **your pet peeves** about how workshops are managed? Think about things like dirty glasses left to sit on tables, or uncomfortable chairs. How can you prevent these pet peeves?

> *" When my reading vision started to decline, I noticed the number of times people in workshops forgot their reading glasses. They either shared with others or were too proud to acknowledge their limitation and simply could not read their notes. Now in our regular supplies we carry inexpensive reading glasses without arms – and participants really appreciate them. "*

✓ Determine if there is **a risk** to health, safety or security. These risks may require an emergency response that supercedes the agenda.

> *" During afternoon break, participants were not aware that an individual was escorted by our staff to the hospital with chest pains. At the end of the workshop we were able to announce that he would be resting quietly overnight there and he wanted everyone to know that he was fine. "*

✓ **Keep improvising,** even in the face of potentially life-threatening situations.

> *" At our hotel, the fire alarm came on five minutes before our break with an announcement to clear the hotel. We not only cleared the building, we went to a restaurant across the street that had windows overlooking the hotel. Once a round of refreshments was ordered, we returned to our discussion topic. Later, when I saw people moving back into the hotel, we headed back to our meeting room. The participants commented more on enjoying the walk than on the emergency situation itself. "*

✓ If **equipment breaks down,** ask yourself:[5]
   - Can you or someone else repair it?
   - Can you replace it? Borrow it? Share it? Buy it?
   - Can you improvise?
   - What is there around you that might work as a substitute?

> *" When my watch stopped half-way through our timed activity, I stole a few glances at participants' watches until our lunch break. Then I went to the mall under the facility, had the battery replaced and returned in time to join everyone for lunch This way I didn't distract people. "*

---

5. Reitz, Helen L. and Marilyn Manning. *The One Stop Guide to Workshops*. New York, p. 279. Adapted.

B. Locations

Decisions about workshop location can have a long-ranging impact on what you get out of a session. These decisions also colour how participants feel about a session over the long term.

Sometimes the best appointed and most attractive sites aren't the best locations for some types of workshops.

> *"We held last year's workshop at a luxury ski resort. Participants loved the location and it was excellent in terms of relaxation and de-stressing. However, attendance was lower than usual at optional sessions and people commented on their evaluation forms that there were a lot of distractions both during and after sessions that were too tempting to resist. People did not rate the workshop highly in terms of what was accomplished."*

Because the workshop site and process are interdependent, it takes careful planning about location to provide the best possible setting for participants.

TIPS

✓ Given the purpose of the workshop, what **message** do you want your location to send to people? Do you want to say:
- this is an urgent and essential meeting: we are here to work?
- this is a perk for your excellent sales efforts: we will have a couple of short meetings and the rest of the time is yours?
- this is an important workshop for top level people who expect the best in service and accommodations?
- this workshop is to help us develop better communication skills; the setting isn't as important as a clear commitment from everyone to address justice issues in our country?

✓ Give some consideration to **perceptions and values**. Does a location favour or benefit a particular individual or interest group? Should the meeting locale be changed or rotated among a number of locations?

Sometimes settings can be **political**. If a city council or a not-for-profit organization holds its retreat on a cruise ship or in a luxurious setting, they leave themselves open to criticism about how they spend tax payers' dollars. On the other hand, a board of directors for a golf club may be seen to be astute by arranging to exchange locations with another golf club at no cost.

✓ Do you want people to enjoy the **distractions** of a busy, downtown hotel location or do you want them to be more **isolated** in a retreat situation?

Part II: Tips, Tools and Templates

✓ Sometimes a **difficult or inadequate** location and room can actually contribute to group development. Participants unite against the challenges in the setting.

> *"When I was facilitating a workshop at a remote fishing resort, the computer presentation wouldn't project, and there was no photocopier available for hard copies. So I drew the diagrams on flip charts as I was talking. People ended up enjoying this less formal approach. We also had a few good laughs about my drawing skills and it helped us all relax."*

✓ **Too much or too little space** in a workshop room are both problematic. Be specific with the location manager about exactly how much space you want.

> *"We will be having a consensus building session with 15 people. I need a room that is large enough to accommodate a hexagon set-up with three people per side except for the front table which is for the facilitator only. The tables can touch at the corners because we don't need to access the centre space. Everyone needs to have eye contact with everyone else. People need space to spread out papers in front of them without feeling cramped.*
>
> *We need space for two flip charts at the front plus a screen angled at one side and space for a data projector that is accessible by the facilitator. The facilitator wants her computer on her right on her table at the front.*
>
> *We will also need space for three round tables at the back of the room, with five chairs per table and about 12-15 feet (3.5-4.5 metres) between tables and wall space for posting flip charts."*

✓ Include information about the session **location and parking** on the workshop agenda.

✓ Check for potential **noise** near the plenary room and surrounding passageways: are the nearby floors tiled or carpeted?

✓ A **hospitality** suite or an area where participants can gather informally has benefits in situations where you want to encourage communication and networking.

✓ **Room temperature** is a common source of discussion, opinion and concern at workshops. If people are too warm or too cold they find it hard to maintain concentration. Given that some workshops have a wide variety of people and clothing styles in the room, find out what the best temperature is for effective work and then talk to those managing the workshop location about room temperature prior to the session. Ask the room maintenance people to keep the room within three degrees of your target temperature.

- ✓ Find out who is participating in the session and set the room temperature to **support their comfort**.
  - If you are convening a one-day meeting of older adults, they will likely be more comfortable in a slightly warmer room than usual.
  - If you are holding a team development session with fitness buffs, keep the room cooler to accommodate active stretch breaks and lunch-time runs.
  - If you are holding a training session for massage therapists who will be practising on each other during the afternoons, find out what the ideal temperature is from the chief therapist.
  - If everyone at your workshop is likely to be wearing three-piece woolen business suits in the middle of winter, set the temperature on the cool side.

- ✓ Profile the session **location's attractiveness**, especially for visitors, e.g., note the historical or cultural significance; feature a range of local artists, offer guided tours during free time.

- ✓ If the session is **being held mid-winter on a dull weekend**, use bright colours in the room to perk up the setting: coloured handouts, highlighter pens and markers, sticky notes, spring flowers.

- ✓ After deciding on the number of participants, select **a venue** that is slightly larger than what you need so that if you end up with more people than anticipated you will be able to accommodate them.

Part II: Tips, Tools and Templates

Tool 6.7

Site Visit Checklist

Whether you visit a site in person or check it out over the phone or by computer, asking the right questions can prevent a lot of potential challenges. Circle all that apply.

The Basics

1. Does the location have the right size and type of space you want to accommodate the number of participants? Think about both plenary and break-out rooms.

2. Does the location have the right ambience for the type of session you are organizing?

3. Is the location accessible for all participants?

4. How convenient is the location in terms of travel?
   - Is public transportation available?
   - Will you need to provide transportation to and from the location, e.g., from airports, train and bus stations?
   - How much time will it take participants to get to and from the workshop site and their workplace, home or hotel?

5. What are the building's opening and closing hours? Do we have to enter or leave the building at a certain time?

6. Do they have an on-site person who will support the workshop requirements and issues?

Safety and Security

7. How safe is the location, e.g., can participants walk and drive without fear for their safety?

8. If safety is an issue, what type of security should we have in place so that participants feel comfortable in this location?

9. Will participants be able to leave their briefcases, computers and coats in the workshop room while they go to another room or location for lunch?

10. When are personnel available to open and lock up the location?

11. Can you recommend some interesting walking tours and jogging paths where participants will feel comfortable getting some fresh air?

12. Where can people park their cars? Is the area lit and patrolled regularly?

13. Will people not in our workshop be able to walk around near the rooms we are using?

14. If breaks and lunch are in the hall outside the main room, how do you ensure that they are not consumed by others not associated with your group?

15. What does the building insurance policy cover with respect to theft?

16. How do we lock up the room when we aren't there, e.g., meals, breaks, end of day?

17. Is the room being used by anyone else in the evenings when we aren't there? If not, can the flipchart, posters and other materials be left in the room from one session to the next, from day to day?

Amenities

18. How does your site handle nutrition and stretch breaks, e.g., in the room, outside of the room, kitchen available, bring-your-own?

19. Where are the washrooms?

20. How much flexibility is there for catering, e.g., vegetarian options, food preferences, allergies?

21. Are there daycare options in the building or nearby? Is there room available nearby where children could play under supervision? Are there toys and games available?

22. What recreational opportunities are available on site or nearby?

Personal Comfort

23. How are the rooms heated and/or ventilated? Can we control the room temperature ourselves?

24. Where are the heating and air conditioning vents?

25. What temperature do you keep your rooms at when this number of people are involved?

26. What options for chairs do you have with a group this size?

27. Do you have two or three adjustable chairs available for people with back problems?

28. Are there other activities taking place nearby at the same time which might be noisy or distracting?

29. What recreational services do you have available?

30. Do you have a hospitality suite that we could make available round the clock?

C. Layouts

Completing the Diagnostic Framework in Chapter 2 will give you important information (e.g., purpose and objectives, type of session, description, participation, presentations, context) that affects how you set up the workshop rooms. As you complete the Diagnostic Framework, your requirements for room layouts will become more obvious.

TIPS

✓ Select your room layout with the **type of workshop** (see Chapter 2) in mind. Is eye contact important? Do people need to be able to see speakers clearly? What role does small group discussion play in achieving the workshop outcomes?

✓ What degree of **formality** is required? Room set-ups for more formal sessions are usually different than those that are informal.

✓ Have one **extra chair** available for every ten people in the session. Put them in an unobtrusive part of the room.

✓ Decisions to open or close **curtains or blinds** depend on:
  - the feeling in the room: does it feel too small, too large, just right, claustrophobic?
  - the degree of distraction: if a large group of animated people are making a movie outside your building and participants can see what is happening, close the curtains. If participants look out on a peaceful woodland scene, you may want to keep the curtains open.
  - the degree of impact the light, heat or cold will have on participants: Does glare from the morning sun hit participants in their eyes? What effect does having the curtains open or closed have on the room temperature?

  You may need to adjust curtains or blinds during a session: if possible, involve participants in these decisions by asking what they prefer.

Logistics, Locations and Layouts

- ✓ Think about the **seasons**. If it's summer, start at a slightly cooler temperature (70-72 degrees F) so that body heat warms the room naturally. If the meeting room has large windows, close the blinds or curtains to reduce the sun's heat.

- ✓ Find out how to open and close the **room door**: does it stay open by pushing it to an extreme position or do you need a door stop?

- ✓ When choosing tables, **be specific** about the size of table that suits your needs. Some sites have small, medium and large round tables as well as 4-foot, 6-foot, 8-foot and 10-foot rectangular tables.

> *We want participants to work in small groups in between watching presentations so we would like to have them at medium round tables with five people per table seated in half-rounds facing the front. Everyone needs to be able to see both screens.*

- ✓ Avoid **pillars** in spaces. No matter what the salesperson tells you, pillars in rooms are problematic. If you can't avoid a pillar or two, make sure that the space in the room where you will have plenary sessions does not have any pillars. This means that space behind the pillar can be used for breakout tables or coffee breaks but can't be considered part of what you require for plenary.

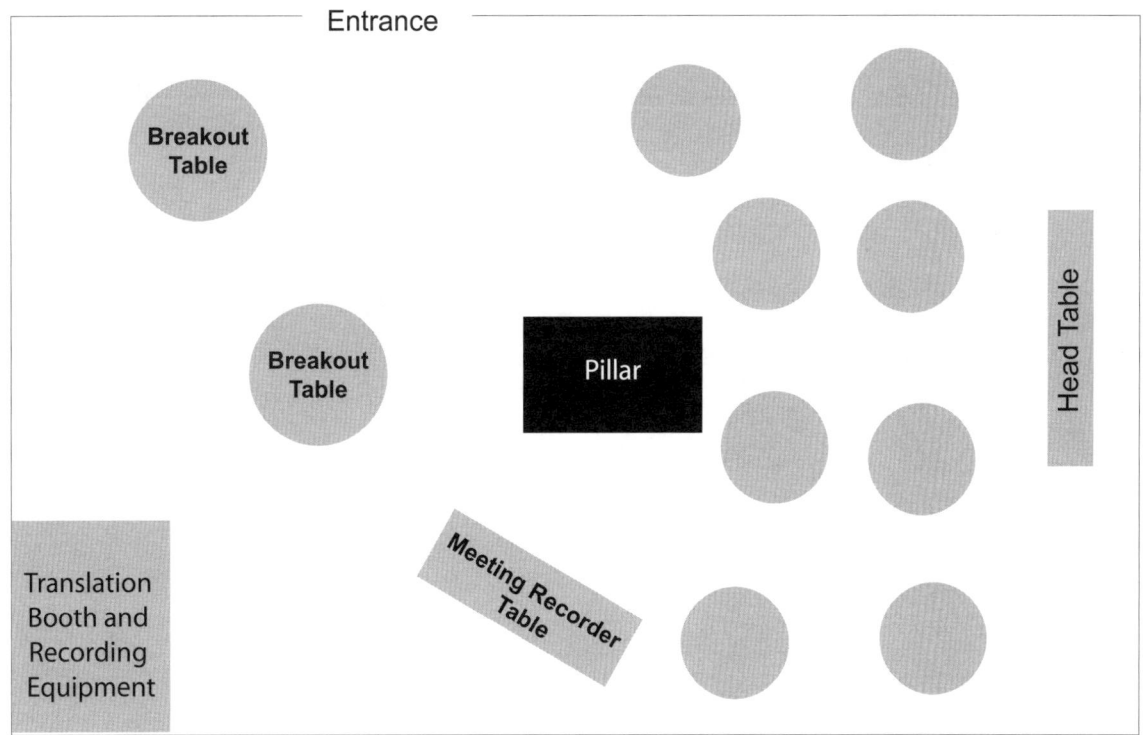

✓ Set up your room to **match the requirements** in the Diagnostic Framework for this session (Chapter 2).
- What is the ideal number of participants in the session?
- Do participants require lots of eye contact, e.g., in support of effective decision making?
- How much room do people need for background papers and handouts?
- Do people need tables for note taking?
- Do you need exhibit space or a couple of long tables where participants can put resources?
- How much personal space do you want people to have? Do you want a cozy friendly tone or a more distanced and reflective kind of tone?
- What are the sightlines to the front of the room like?
- To what extent do you want the room set-up to encourage interaction among participants?
- How much space do you want between participant and head tables?
- Do you need rooms for breakout sessions?

Tool 6.8

Room Layouts

L = Low; M = Medium; H = High

Shape	Ideal Number	Eye Contact	Room for Papers	Note Taking	Sightline to Front	Personal Space	Interaction Potential	Tips
Round Tables	5 to 12 depending on size of table	H at table	H if table large enough	H	H if people are facing front	H if table large enough	H	• Good layout for a Roundtable where you want everyone to have equal status
Boardroom	3 per side + 1 at front = 10	H if no more than 3 per side; M or L if large #'s	H	H	M or H if front of room is unobstructed	H if table large enough	H if no more than 3 per side; M or L if large #'s	• Common for formal setting involving a chairperson • If more people involved inhibits communication and interaction
U-Shape	2 or 3 per side so that everyone can see everyone else	H if no more than 3 per side	H depending on length of tables	H depending on length of tables	H if no more than 3 per side and screen and tables on an angle	H	H if no more than 3 per side	
Diamond (4 sides) Pentagon (5 sides) Hexagon (6 sides)								• A great set-up for decision-making sessions that require maximum eye contact • Leave space between the tables if you want to walk into the centre • Put a chair on the inside of each table and you have an instant small group set-up

Part II: Tips, Tools and Templates

L = Low; M = Medium; H = High

Shape	Ideal Number	Eye Contact	Room for Papers	Note Taking	Sightline to Front	Personal Space	Interaction Potential	Tips
Rectangular Tables in Alternate Formation — Front	5 or 6 per table, depending on length of tables	M or L if tables face front and people are looking at others' backs	H	H	H if everyone facing front	H depending on size of tables	H at tables; M or L for rest of room	• Can't get as many people involved as with round tables but also works well • Some sites have narrow rectangular tables – avoid using these if there is a lot of paper involved • Depending on the length of tables, people sitting at the ends may not be able to hear well and may feel left out
Round Tables in Semi-Circular Formation — Front	6 to 8 per table depending on diameter of tables	H at tables; M with rest of room if in semicircle	H	H	H if people are seated in half rounds with everyone facing front	M to H depending on number of people at table	H	• Works well with groups of 40–200 where you need lots of interaction • Number the tables for easy identification during plenary sessions
Theatre — Front	Depends on size of theatre and purpose of session	L only with one person on each side	L if arm for writing; often none	L if arm for writing; often none	H	L although movable chairs may improve this	L or none	• Works best for lectures and presentations where speaker is more concerned with teaching than learning

Logistics, Locations and Layouts

L = Low; M = Medium; H = High

Shape	Ideal Number	Eye Contact	Room for Papers	Note Taking	Sightline to Front	Personal Space	Interaction Potential	Tips
Classroom	Depends on purpose of session and size of room	H at each table if no more than 3 per side; L if large #'s and chairs don't swivel	M to H depending on the size of tables	H	M to H depending on # of people	H if tables large enough	H at tables; M or L for rest of room	• Common for formal settings involving a chairperson • Large numbers inhibit communication and interaction
Circle of Chairs	Depends on purpose of session and size of room	M to H depending on number in the circle	L to none	L to none	Varies depending on how the front is used	L	L to H depending on size of circle	• Many people feel vulnerable in this setting. There is nothing physical to lean on • Assumes that participants don't have paper and/or don't want to take notes
Lounge	8 to 12	H	M depending on room set-up, e.g., side and coffee tables	M	Front of room not usually important in these sessions	M to H	H	• Good setting for informal discussions such as book clubs, or to explore topics for lengthy periods of time • Less appropriate for focused desicion making

6

Chapter 7

Speakers

★★★★★★★★★★★★★★★★★★★★★★★

★★★★★★★★★★★★★★★★★★★★★★★

Speakers

Effective speakers advance the purpose of a workshop by providing the right message, at the right time, in the right tone and language for participants.

Workshop facilitators/managers can enable speakers to support workshop objectives in many ways: they can prepare draft opening and closing remarks for speakers to customize; they can provide information about participant expectations and what will be going on before and after a presentation; they can also brief speakers on how their presentations can help support session objectives.

This chapter provides tips, tools and templates for facilitators working with speakers in four situations:

A. Opening Remarks

B. Presentations by Experts

C. Panel Presentations

D. Closing Remarks.

The focus throughout this chapter is on how you can work with speakers in support of the workshop purpose and objectives. Legal aspects – such as formal letters of contract with speakers – are not included in this approach.[1]

---

1. For examples of formal contracts with speakers, see Howard L. Shenson. *How to Develop and Promote Successful Seminars and Workshops.* Toronto: John Wiley & Sons, Inc., 1990.

A. Opening Remarks

Opening remarks set the tone for a workshop. Once you have completed a Workshop Diagnostic Framework (Chapter 2) you will know who needs to say what to get the workshop off on the right foot.

METHOD TO MAGIC

Diagnostic: You are managing a two-day training workshop for customer service (CS) representatives in a retail business. This workshop is the first one of three sessions to be held bi-monthly. New owners have targeted CS, which has been rated low for the past few years, for improvement. Half the workshop participants are newly appointed CS representatives and are enthusiastic about their new positions. The other half have been with the company for several years, and are cynical about new approaches, given their shabby treatment by previous owners.

Decisions: The opening speaker is the new Vice President, CS. He welcomes people, gives a rationale for the workshop and describes current challenges facing the company and its new owners.

The VP introduces a new incentive plan for CS bonuses and new expectations and values for how CS will be delivered. He closes his presentation by explaining that the company sees the participants in this workshop as its internal customers and will treat them accordingly, following the new CS values. Participants complete a CS evaluation form at the end of the session. The results are summarized and changes integrated into how the next session is managed.

I felt comfortable at this session right from the get-go. Things were well organized by the planning committee and they went out of their way to make us feel welcome. Having the VP start things off was a great idea – he was positive, but he also laid down the law and didn't do any blaming. I think he really cares. What surprised me the most was that in the workshop they acted on all the things they expect us to do on a day-to-day basis. There was a lot of respect and good service going around. One guy actually got his room changed because the air conditioner was too loud.

This workshop got off on the right foot because the opening remarks were on target and were also supported by how the workshop was managed. The facilitator and opening speaker had worked closely with the workshop manager to ensure that there were no contradictions between the values the Vice-President of CS was espousing and what participants experienced in the session.[2] Participants were treated with the same respect and attention to detail that they were expected to deliver to the company's customers.

TIPS

✓ Select speakers who **fit the type of workshop**[3] you are managing. If you are facilitating a roundtable (where participants share equal influence and status and where no single point of view is being pushed), your choice of opening speaker(s) will set the tone for the workshop. Choose someone who can be even-handed and won't use his authority to drive a specific perspective. If you are facilitating a training session for workplace diversity sponsors, select an opening speaker who is respected in the community and has had some success promoting advocacy in his own workplace.

✓ Think carefully about **requirements** for your opening speaker:
  - Do you require someone who brings credibility to the workshop topic or themes?
  - Do you need someone with a commitment to changing the status quo based on decisions expected during the session?
  - Does the session require a person of authority to give the event legitimacy?

> *" Welcome! I have been anticipating making these opening remarks for several months now. All the background information we gathered, all the brainstorming sessions and focus groups we held, all the late afternoon coffee shop sessions ... all of these have been building towards this consolidation session. I am looking forward to taking the results of these discussions to our executive committee meeting tomorrow afternoon for some final decisions. "*

---

2. See Chapter 3, "Decision Making," for guidelines on making decisions in support of the diagnostic framework.
3. See Chapter 2, "A Diagnostic Framework," and Chapter 3, "Decision Making," for more information on types of workshops.

Part II: Tips, Tools and Templates

✓ Many workshops have more than one speaker providing opening remarks. When this is the case, think carefully about the **order of speakers**.

> *" In one large, high profile workshop that the media followed closely, we started with a general welcome from a prominent local politician. Then a senior volunteer in a sponsoring organization talked about the importance of the session for providing strategic direction to her organization. She finished on a lighter note by drawing two door prizes related to the workshop theme. Then a credible content expert reviewed the results of a pre-workshop questionnaire. The pacing and order of speakers worked well for this session. "*

✓ Consider developing opening remarks through the following **steps**:
   - Ask the opening speaker if she would like you to suggest some key points for her remarks. Explain the need for links between what she says at the outset of the process, what will happen immediately afterward and then throughout the agenda and in closing remarks. Ask what format she would like, e.g., a few key words, some main points, a detailed script.
   - Refer to the results of the Workshop Diagnostic Framework in Chapter 2.
   - Ask the client or session planning committee for ideas for opening remarks.
   - Develop opening remarks based on the W7 framework (see next page) as a guide.
   - Send initial draft opening remarks to the speaker, asking for her feedback or leaving them with her to finalize.
   - If it's appropriate, revise and finalize the remarks and return them to the speaker. Encourage her to speak without reading from her notes and to feel free about making changes, additions, etc., up until delivery time.

✓ Don't staple the pages of the speaker's opening remarks – the **pages rustle** and this noise can be distracting, especially if the speaker is using a microphone.

✓ When you are drafting opening remarks, ask the speaker which **writing approach** she prefers, e.g., point-form key words or phrases or a complete, full sentence script.

✓ Be clear about the **values** the organizing committee wants to project in the opening remarks. Can you refer to something in a mission statement or ground rules or organizational guiding principles that will anchor the opening remarks?

Opening Speakers: W7

One way to outline opening remarks is to think about the following W7 Checklist and decide which elements to include to ensure your process gets off to a good start.

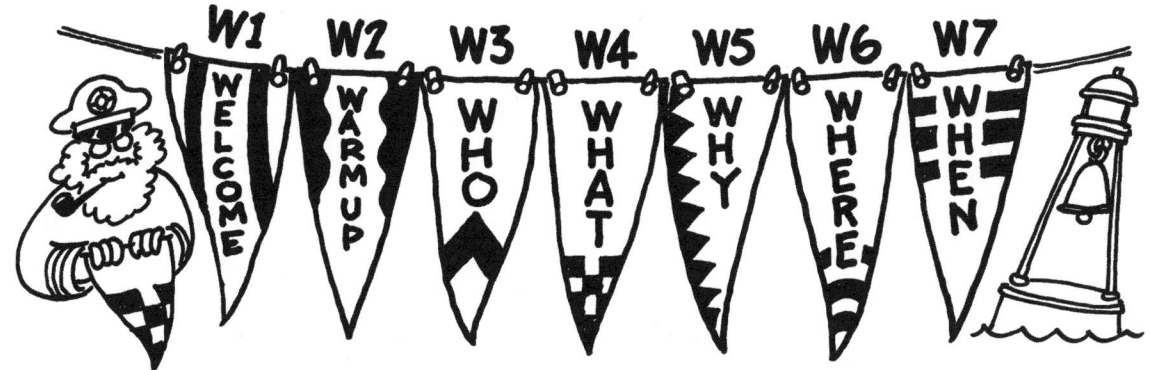

1. **Welcome:** greetings, value of participation

2. **Warm-up:** history, importance of, and confidence in, the process; values

3. **Who:** participants and planners, backgrounds and acknowledgements

4. **What:** activities

5. **Why:** purpose and expected outcomes

6. **Where:** why this location

7. **When:** why now

Use the Workshop Diagnostic Framework in Chapter 2 as a guide for selecting which W7 items you want in your opening remarks and which of those you want to emphasize. If you are managing a team development session for a national sports team prior to the Olympics, then you may want to suggest that the opening speaker focus on W2 - Warm-up + W3 - Participants + W5 - Purpose and Expected Outcomes. If you are facilitating a large national sales training workshop, then you may want the opening speaker to focus on W1 - Welcome + W2 - Warm-up.

1. Welcome

The initial welcoming part of opening remarks assures people that their participation is valued and helps create a comfortable climate for working together.

> *A heartfelt welcome to everyone – all 16 of us – who gave up a family weekend to work together on this important policy agenda against poverty. On behalf of all the people in our region, I thank you for contributing your energy and ideas over the next couple of days.*

Some opening remarks, such as for a conference of professionals or at a summit on environmental change, celebrate the attendance of people in a very prominent and visible manner, e.g., with banners, music and a lot of fanfare. Other opening remarks are low key. They put people at ease, assure people that their input is essential and invite them to be candid, patient and forthcoming in discussions.

> *Good morning and a warm welcome to everyone. Our focus today during this session is on the possible. We are here to generate new ideas and develop partnerships so that we can improve how our technology processes can support you – the engineers – better.*
>
> *We will no doubt go through some confusing discussions. However, as one wit said, "if you are not confused you are just not thinking clearly." So I'm looking forward to a very confusing morning with all of you.*

2. Warm-up

The opening speaker begins to warm up the group. This involves providing some history, getting ideas flowing, building enthusiasm, showing confidence and encouraging involvement and commitment. Just as a physical warm-up prepares the body to do strenuous work, so the process warm-up prepares a group to collaborate to achieve specific outcomes based on key values.

> *Most speakers start out by saying "thank you" for coming to sessions like this one. I'm not going to do that because in this situation it would be condescending. This planning session is one of the most important things we can do to ensure the success of our corporation; and in addition to the fact that it's going to be a stimulating and exciting day for all of us – everyone in this room is paid to be here! Life doesn't get much better.*
>
> *We are here today because we need to help each other reach some common goals. So no "thank yous." We're in this together.*

3. Who

Opening speakers usually acknowledge and thank people for the time and energy it takes for them to participate in a session.

Participants in workshops often wonder how well they fit with others around them. By describing who is present and why their participation is valued, the opening speaker can address any discomfort related to inclusion. This helps to reduce anxiety and supports participants in beginning to build ownership for the outcomes of a session.

> *If you look around this room you will notice that we have invited people with a wide variety of backgrounds and experience. We wanted to have professionals, volunteers, students, parents and advocates present to ensure that we are including as many perspectives as possible during this initial phase of our deliberations. Your voice is important: please speak up and participate wholeheartedly.*

4. What

It works well if the opening speaker describes in general terms what people are going to do and leaves the specific objectives and outcomes to the facilitator.

> *I have been looking forward to this day ever since the seed money came in to support us in developing our research potential. Today's session will provide us with an opportunity to learn from the experience of other organizations and then to use what we learn to enhance our own research initiatives here at Sound Enterprises. And we all know the importance of research for improving the quality of music we deliver every day.*

People come to sessions with their own hopes and concerns. They hope to hear about new ideas, but they may worry that the workshop will waste their time, or that the outcome has been pre-determined. The opening speaker can address these hopes and concerns by assuring participants about the integrity of the process. He can also highlight the main segments of the agenda and what people will leave with at the end.

> *Thank you for sending in your needs assessments. As you know, your facilitator for today prepared a summary of your comments for the planning committee and that summary was very helpful in developing today's agenda. All five members of the planning committee are keen to hear what you have to say. We are not wedded to any particular outcome. We have an external facilitator with us here today whose role is to ensure that the process is productive, fun and un-biased; she is not a content expert.*

5. Why

By addressing why an event is being held, the opening speaker provides a context for the session and begins to focus the event. The "why" part of her opening remarks can also put tensions on the table in a constructive and open manner.

> *I need your help. Our industry is changing at a speed that no one could ever have imagined. And although it's true that we are perceived to be the foremost thought leader when it comes to the Internet, maintaining that reputation requires the constant maximizing of our creative potential. And that's why the 12 of us are here this weekend. We are here to think. To play. To generate options. To make the future come alive in our hands.*

Being transparent about the rationale for an event helps build credibility for the final product.

> *I know that there is some cynicism about examining efficiencies on sales accounts. And that is understandable – because most of us here today are more interested in being out there actively closing deals than being in here thinking about the financial details.*
>
> *But that perspective in itself can be dangerous. Because if we don't pay attention to cost benefit analysis and leverage our high impact sales activities, we will lose our edge. And that leads to an inefficient sales force rather than a targeted and dynamic one.*
>
> *Our numbers are down for this quarter and our customers are telling us that we don't seem focused. It's time for us to leverage our strengths and offset our inefficiencies with respect to the way we work together.*

Sometimes leaders in an organization set up a session because they want to give participants a wake-up call.

> *This session is a wake-up call for all of us. In three months we will be out of money and there are no new funds on the horizon. This is nothing new: we have been in this position several times over the past ten years. However, this time things are slightly different. Governments are cutting back on funds for organizations like ours and corporate donations are dwindling.*
>
> *We need a new strategy to ensure that we are still functioning and able to be productive this time next year.*

Other times, the fiscal situation is just fine and the purpose of a session is to get creative juices going to stimulate new ideas.

> *We are here this morning to have some fun. This is a brainstorming session so our focus is on being creative, on generating alternatives, on stretching boundaries and thinking outside of the proverbial box. And over the next three hours we will do just that – have fun. We don't need to come to conclusions and to develop action plans. We have some of the best brains in our organization in the room and our focus is on generating ideas for new products.*

6. Where

Where an event is held is a consideration for both clients and participants. By providing a rationale for the location you assure participants that you have been thinking about their preferences and needs in relation to the setting.

> *We are having this conference at a downtown location so that you can enjoy all the great benefits of this wonderful city: a wide variety of fine foods, an interesting market area to explore on foot and a great waterfront for walking and boat tours.*

7. When

Most sessions are held at a certain time of year or month for a specific reason that has an impact on outcomes. Being clear about the timing of a session can address concerns that participants may have regarding how they plan their own work and personal lives.

> *I know that holding this session now may be an added hardship for some of you because this is our busiest time of the year. However, that being said, we have had some new developments in our product line and we need to ensure that we are up and running with these products within three weeks.*

TEMPLATE 7.1
OUTLINE FOR OPENING REMARKS FOR A NATIONAL RESEARCH WORKSHOP

Speaker: President of the Research Institute

WELCOME – thank you for attending (W1 + W3)

HISTORY – of this event (W2)

APPROACH TO RESEARCH – "integrative" approach, values (W2 + W5)

OUR MANDATE – why we are doing this (W5)

COLLABORATIVE PARTNERSHIPS – lessons learned (W3 + W5)

IDEALISM AND REALISM – we need both (W2 + W5)

PARTICIPATE FREELY – commitments later (W1 + W4)

STEERING COMMITTEE for this event – a partnership (W1 + W3)

OVER TO FACILITATOR – objectivity (W4 + W5)

TEMPLATE 7.2

OPENING REMARKS FOR A NATIONAL RESEARCH WORKSHOP

Speaker: President of the Research Institute

WELCOME

- on behalf of the workshop steering committee, warm welcome
- key initiative for all of us here – time to think about opportunities
- we are doing this session at one of our central research facilities to ease transportation and give us an opportunity for a learning tour – hope you find this enjoyable.

HISTORY

- this forum is the second in a series focused on building a framework for effective partnering in support of research and training in . . .
- the first forum, held a year ago this month, began to lay a foundation for these collaborative relationships
- we plan to hold annual partnership events at the same time each year as it fits well with our funding timelines
- the purpose of this second forum is to build on that foundation and begin to develop an integrative strategic research agenda among national groups and organizations involved in . . . .

APPROACH TO RESEARCH

- by integrative, we mean research initiatives across disciplines, sectors and regions that combine into an interrelated whole – a collaborative approach that is central to our organizational values
- brings together several components, elements or approaches formerly regarded as separate
- reflects the emerging health needs of our citizens
- the integrative part is what makes this fun.

OUR MANDATE

- this forum is a good example of our organization's mandate to coordinate and facilitate research initiatives in the area of . . . .
- we're here as an equal player looking for partnerships, but we also have an additional mandate to enable partnerships.

COLLABORATIVE PARTNERSHIPS

- we've come a long way in terms of partnerships in an integrative agenda
- we've learned that partnerships can be an effective way to capitalize on limited research capacity by pooling resources
- there is no creativity without limits; we all share resource and financial limits to some extent – our job is to be creative within those limits
- there are three possible levels of involvement in potential partnerships: partner, adjunct partner and observer-learner
- each organization here is at a different stage of partner development
- on some initiatives you may want to be a partner and on others an adjunct partner; you may also decide you aren't ready to partner at all and that's fine too
- need to be open to a variety of ways for how you could be involved.

IDEALISM AND REALISM

- one lesson learned: partners need to be both idealistic and realistic
- need for candor regarding how we work together: this makes a partnership go well or go poorly
- rarely problem with content or science – almost always process issues such as ownership, boundaries, personalities
- we will be exploring some of these challenges during this workshop
- at the same time we need to keep our eye on our dreams – the idealistic part
- working together takes work – the work pays off
- rewards can be very worthwhile – ideals can be realized.

PARTICIPATE FREELY

- we recognize that it may not be possible for you to commit your organization to anything today – participation in the forum is completely "without prejudice"
- however, we do hope that when you have a chance to discuss the results of the forum with your organization, you will do so positively; what we want to do here is set in motion a process that will lead to partnering with one or more organizations
- what we ask of you today and tomorrow is your good will, an open mind, and an optimistic nature.

STEERING COMMITTEE
- a partnership organized this event
- introduce steering committee members and thank them (W 3)
- introduce the facilitator: final comment on objectivity in her role (W3 + W4)

OVER TO FACILITATOR

Tool 7.3

Outline for Opening Remarks for a Regional Sales Meeting

Speaker: Regional Director of Sales

The Workshop Diagnostic Framework (Chapter 2) helps you to determine which aspects of W7 need to be emphasized during opening remarks. Because the following template is for a regional sales team meeting, the speaker emphasizes:

- W2 - Warm-up
- W3 - Who is on the team
- W5 - Why outcomes matter.

WELCOME – great to be here again (W1 + W3)

CELEBRATION – goals and achievements (W2 + W5 + W7)

COPORATE GOALS – what head office expects (W2 + W5)

TEAM STRENGTHS, CHALLENGES – related to goals (W2 + W3 + W5)

IMPORTANCE OF TEAM SYNERGY (W2 + W3 + W5)

FOCUS AND TECH ETIQUETTE – (W2 + W4 + W6)

OVER TO FACILITATOR – objectivity (W3 + W4)

Template 7.4
Opening Remarks for a Regional Sales Meeting

WELCOME

- great to be here doing this planning session
- I'm counting on this session to give us a strong sense of direction over the coming year.

CELEBRATION

- goals and achievements
- 3 key successes over the past year.

CORPORATE GOALS

- what head office expects over the coming year
- you heard about new goals for our region last week
- they are formidable but do-able.

STRENGTHS, CHALLENGES

- in relation to revised corporate goals
- we are good at being responsive
- not so good at future scenarios
- today is about the future.

IMPORTANCE OF TEAM

- synergy: 2 + 2 = 5
- industry experiencing lots of turnover
- important to spend time with each other, becoming more familiar
- need for team mind-share if we are to reach our goals
- the expertise is in this room to do the work.

FOCUS AND TECH ETIQUETTE

- know you want to be available for customers so holding this in-house
- we have instructed reception to inform callers about this workshop
- we will have 30 minute breaks every 1.5 hours so you will have time to check in
- please turn off all phones, pagers, computers, etc.

OVER TO FACILITATOR
- a lot of informal planning discussions throughout the year
- this one is different – part of the corporate planning process
- facilitator gives us an objective perspective and also takes over the management of this off-site session
- please welcome her.

B. Presentations by Experts

Expert speakers are a frequent highlight at workshops. You can support them to deliver great presentations by ensuring that they are engaged and aligned with the workshop purpose and agenda.

- Speakers who are **engaged** in a workshop topic area have a commitment to contributing to the topic: they have a keen interest in it and want to work with others who share their enthusiasm for the area.

- Speakers who are **aligned** with a workshop agenda agree to harmonize their presentation with the session purpose and objectives to better enable participants to achieve expected outcomes.

Most speakers want to be well received. If you support them in making a meaningful contribution to the purpose of a workshop, they can in turn support participants in working through the agenda successfully.

TIPS

✓ Use your diagnostic framework to select **speakers who fit the type of workshop**[4] you are managing. If you want a keynote speaker for a roundtable, select someone who can present a range of perspectives on the workshop topic without driving any single point of view. Or if it's a training session for community environmental advocates, pick panel members who have experience in the area and can motivate participants to stay focused and involved throughout a potentially lengthy advocacy process.

✓ Expert speakers are contracted to satisfy **two clients:** (a) the person or planning committee hiring them to do the presentation, and (b) the session participant listening to their ideas. Regardless of whether the speaker is paid or not, he is in service to both of these clients and has an obligation to ensure that his remarks reflect his engagement and alignment with the workshop purpose and agenda.

✓ Be clear with your speaker about the **purpose of her presentation** and how her expertise can meet clients' needs and contribute to workshop outcomes. Is the purpose to provide background information or an historical context? Is it to give an overview of the current situation, outline a specific perspective, explain a concept, generate discussion and controversy, or advocate for a point of view? The more clarity you provide the speaker regarding the purpose of the presentation, the greater the likelihood that she can customize her remarks to meet her clients' needs.

---

4. See Chapter 2, "A Diagnostic Framework," and Chapter 3, "Decision Making," for more information on types of workshops.

✓ Guest speakers often have **canned presentations** that they deliver to a wide variety of audiences. More often than not, these generic approaches are also wide of the mark. Ask your speaker if she is planning on using a presentation that she has delivered elsewhere. If the answer is yes, go through the presentation with her to determine how engaged she is with the topic area and whether her approach and content are aligned with the session objectives.

✓ Don't let **"big name" speakers** skew an agenda. Instead, harness the speaker's energy and expertise to support your objectives.

With the evolution of information technology, the role of guest speakers has changed considerably. Where previously most workshop participants wanted to see and hear the "big names" on a particular topic, these days many such presentations are easily attainable on the Web or through bookstores. Today the demand is increasingly for meaningful interaction resulting in personal insights and applied learning.

> *Most learning events still string a list of speakers together and use question-and-answer periods as a way of involving participants.*
>
> *People who plan the events at which I speak ask me only three questions: when will I arrive, what kind of microphone do I want, and will I be using flip charts, slides, overheads, or video? I wish planning people would ask me three different questions:*
>   1. *How are you going to engage the audience?*
>   2. *What kind of room would be appropriate for your purpose?*
>   3. *How are you going to assess how it is going?*
>
> *These should be the "larger" questions of how we come together to learn and evoke change. Get these questions right, and who speaks and what they say might be brought back into perspective.*[5]

---

5. Block, Peter and Andrea Markowitz. *The Flawless Consulting Fieldbook and Companion.* San Francisco: Jossey-Bass/Pfeiffer: 2001, 150.

The following example illustrates one approach to meaningful interaction between speakers and participants.

METHOD TO MAGIC

Diagnostic: The workshop is a one day think tank for an architectural firm commissioned to build a state-of-the-art museum in a provincial capital city. Of the 45 workshop participants, fifteen people represent the interests of municipalities within a day's travel of the museum, eight people represent the funders, and ten people are current CEOs of museums elsewhere in the country. Twelve participants are interested citizens without any affiliation.

Museum attendance in the province is at an all time low.

The workshop site is a local museum.

Decisions: The opening speaker is the author of a recent report, "Building Great Museums: What Works and What Doesn't." Participants get the report prior to the workshop. The speaker opens the day with a brief overview of key points from the report and then asks participants to:

(a) prioritize the points in terms of a museum for their city, and

(b) evaluate the workshop site (a local museum) on these points.

After several focused small group activities and related plenary discussions, a three-person panel from the architectural company summarizes what they have heard in relation to the new structure they are planning. Each member of the panel makes a brief presentation on a specific aspect of the building and then checks that he has heard correctly what people have said.

This was a very satisfying day for our group. The organizers had speakers at the beginning and end of the day and even though they were experts, their opinions didn't dominate. I was amazed to find that we were the centre of attention. They listened and took notes about what we said and then actively tried to come up with approaches that would accommodate our perspectives. The experience of having these high-paid experts really listening to us was a new one for me. And after all that, we will have a chance to review the workshop report for accuracy. We're also getting a report from the architectural firm about how they are going to accommodate our ideas. This was an amazingly well-organized session.

✓ Provide an opportunity for workshop participants to reflect on the presentation and how it relates to their purpose and objectives. Critical thinking takes time: people need to test how ideas feel and explore their assumptions and values. Ensure that you have adequate time in your agenda for **critical thinking**.[6]

> *Panel Moderator:*
>
> *"Here are the educational challenges we want to address through this workshop. Keep the criteria for effective solutions to these challenges in front of you and jot down solutions that come to mind as you listen to these expert panel members. After the panel is over, we will be working in small groups to discuss and prioritize solutions for each challenge area."*

✓ Be clear about **timelines** for presentations and then stick to them. When you allow a speaker to take up participants' discussion time, the message is clear, i.e., what the speaker wants to say is more important than what your participants want to discuss.

✓ Distribute **speaker biographies** before or at the workshop – this saves time and encourages brief introductions.

✓ **Avoid contradictions** between the speakers' topics and how the workshop is managed.
  - If the focus of presentations is on high-quality research, ensure that the pre-session questionnaire is of a high quality.
  - If the session is about effective electronic communication, follow the guidelines that speakers will be suggesting in the workshop when you communicate with participants before, during and after the session.
  - If you are facilitating a workshop on heart disease, select healthy meals and schedule activity breaks.
  - If you are convening a session with Olympic athletes who are discussing excessive spending by their administrative bodies, keep this in mind when selecting the venue and arranging transportation.

✓ Depending on the type of workshop and the nature of your speakers, you may want to think about how you can support your speakers to be **authentic**.

> *Authenticity is about being real or genuine. It is about avoiding self-deception, becoming more and more like yourself when working with others.*[7]

---

6. Strachan, Dorothy. *Questions that Work: A Resource for Facilitators.* Ottawa: ST Press, 2001. stpress@cyberus.ca. www.stpress.ca. See this handbook for suggestions on how to encourage critical thinking, p. 35.
7. Ibid.

In addition to providing "hard data," encourage presenters to talk about their personal experience in an area. Ask them to talk about their mistakes as well as their successes and to disclose the challenges and fears they have experienced.

- ✓ Let your speakers know that you want to distribute copies of their presentations to participants and ask them if they have any concerns about **intellectual property rights.**

- ✓ When you have more than one speaker at a session (e.g., on a panel) share **speaker outlines** among presenters to ensure that they don't duplicate one another.

- ✓ If you are putting a summary of a presentation in a workshop report or proceedings, **share a draft version** with speakers to ensure that they are comfortable with what will be published and distributed.

- ✓ Consider all your options when thinking about **compensation.** Which of the following do you want to pay for?
    - registration fee
    - presentation, e.g., honorarium or professional speaker's fee
    - travel and accommodation expenses
    - audiovisual aids, e.g., data projector, overhead projector, flipcharts
    - copies of books
    - handouts for participants

Speakers frequently receive no payment for speaking and no contribution towards travel and accommodation. This approach is common at professional meetings where members of a professional association will be attending the conference or workshop anyway and will benefit from exposure, tenure points at their university or an opportunity to build profile and market publications.

Tool 7.5
Checklist for Managing Expert Speakers

This tool provides a comprehensive list. Choose the items that apply to your workshop and then customize to follow through.

Before the Workshop

1. Brief the speakers on:
   a. Workshop participants, e.g., experience in the topic area, academic background, expectations
   b. How the presentation fits within the session purpose and objectives
   c. How the presentation fits into the agenda, i.e., what participants will be doing before, during and after the presentation; how the presentation will help participants achieve the session outcomes
   d. The purpose of the presentation, e.g., for background information, for skill development, to provide a unique perspective, to encourage advocacy for a point of view
   e. The workshop process: purpose, objectives, outcomes, key assumptions. Ensure that they understand how the agenda flows, how they fit in and what will be happening before and immediately following their presentations. Provide speakers with a list of key terms and acronyms related to the workshop content.

2. Verify the pronunciation of the speaker's name.

3. Ask the speaker if this presentation is one that she has used before. If the answer is "yes," ask what groups have heard this presentation so that she isn't repeating something some of your participants may have already heard. Review the key points in the presentation to ensure that they tie directly into the purpose and outcomes of the workshop.

4. Request a paper copy of slides/overheads so that you can (a) review them for relevance, and (b) distribute them to participants for note-taking during the presentation. Clarify potential copyright issues related to printing this information.

5. Ask for audiovisual aids to be in a specific font and size so that everyone will be able to see. You may want to customize the aids so that they include your organization's logo or so that all speakers have the same background design on slides.

6. Provide water at room temperature within easy reach of speakers.

7. Describe what participants will be doing during presentations, e.g., What will they be listening for? How will they be using information from these presentations during later deliberations?

8. Avoid surprises. Share the results of needs assessments, focus groups, research, etc., with speakers before the workshop. Explore the kinds of questions they may get during discussions.

9. Explain your policy about marketing, e.g., whether the speaker can advertise his books during his talk.

10. Encourage speakers to be explicit in their introductions about how their presentations fit into the workshop objectives and outcomes.

11. Ask the speaker if there are ways that the session could be organized in support of what she is going to say, e.g., if it is a session on global warming, explore what could be done from a management perspective to support the concepts in the presentation.

12. Ask the speaker what she would like to get out of her participation in the session.

13. Document mutual expectations in a letter to speakers. Use the letter as your contract for services. (See the templates provided later in this chapter.)

14. If you will be asking participants to provide feedback on the speaker, share the feedback format and process with the speaker before the workshop. Arrange for a time after the workshop to share a summary of the information received.

During the Workshop

15. When you introduce a speaker:

    a. Explain why you asked this person to come and what you have asked him to talk about

    b. Provide information that supports the speaker's credibility with participants, e.g., the speaker's experience, education, and publications relevant to the purpose and outcomes of the session

    c. If you have one, tell a brief personal anecdote about the speaker

    d. Describe the challenges that workshop participants are facing and how this presentation is intended to address those challenges

    e. Suggest what you would like participants to reflect on during the presentation

    f. Remind participants that copies of the speaker's overheads are either in their kits or on their tables

    g. Tell participants what they will be doing after the presentation, e.g., small group work or plenary discussion

    h. Explain how long the presentation will be and how long the speaker will be at the workshop, e.g., only for the presentation or for the entire workshop so that participants can anticipate how and when they will be able to engage the speaker after the presentation.

16. Provide participants with opportunities to reflect on and discuss what was said during a presentation, e.g., through a discussion period, a small group task, a responding panel, a debate format.

17. When you thank a speaker:
    a. Start with a general comment on the presentation.
    b. Mention something that stood out for you or that you noticed during discussions with participants.
    c. Thank the speaker for her time and effort and her specificity with respect to the workshop objectives.
    d. Give a small gift or token if appropriate, e.g., a pin or pen with the workshop or your organization's name on it.
    e. Build a bridge between what the speaker has said and the next part of your agenda.

After the Workshop

18. Summarize feedback on the presentation and share it with the speaker and the participants.

19. If payment is involved, do it promptly.

Tool 7.6
Commercialism Policies

To prevent confusion and misunderstandings, be clear with speakers about your organization's approach to commercialism in presentations.

> *" Earlier this year, I organized a one-day workshop on strategic alliances in the high-tech sector. We paid a lot of money to a speaker's bureau for a keynote presenter who was a professor at a university in a neighbouring country, about a day's travel away. I didn't mention restrictions on advertising and promotion during discussions with the bureau or later with the speaker. I was horrified when he opened his presentation with slides advertising his two books. He also brought copies with him to sell and handed out bookmarks. At least half of his slides were quotations from these books and he shamelessly promoted his consulting services throughout the entire presentation, e.g., "when I worked with …", or "we often consult with organizations like some of yours who need our services to …" Our participants, who paid significant registration fees, were irritated and offended. "*

If you have a policy on marketing, provide it in writing to speakers. Be specific about what is and is not allowed in relation to your workshop, e.g., naming and discussing work done with other clients, suggesting products, services or solutions to group members, offering publications for sale.

Sample Policies

Excerpt from a letter to expert panel members in a workshop called "What's New in Organizational Design?"

> *Participants in this workshop are aware that panel members are contributing their time as expert speakers in exchange for an opportunity to promote their organization's services in the workshop brochure. Please use the 15 minutes of your panel presentation to focus exclusively on the requested topic area. Do not include the names of clients or in any way promote your organization during the panel process.*
>
> *The people introducing and thanking you will mention your organization's services in their remarks. To this end, please provide us with a 25 word promotional description and we will include this information in their remarks.*

Excerpt from the Speaker's Manual for a Canadian Society of Association Executives[8] (CSAE) national conference.

> CSAE provides a unique opportunity for open dialogue and creative exchange of ideas among association professionals. With this in mind, speakers and facilitators must refrain from the use of brand names or specific product endorsements in their presentations. Under no circumstances is this platform to be used as a place for direct promotion of a speaker's product, service or monetary self-interest.

Excerpt from a Request for Submissions for an annual conference of the International Association of Facilitators.[9]

> Facilitators are invited to promote products and services through the exhibit area or bookstore. Promotion of products or services is not acceptable in conference sessions.

---

8. Canadian Society of Association Executives, 10 King Street East, Suite 1100, Toronto, Ontario M5C 1C3 Canada. 416-363-3555. www.csae.com.

9. International Association of Facilitators, 7630 West 145th Street, Suite 202, St. Paul, Minnesota 55124. 952-891-1800. www.iaf-world.org.

Tool 7.7
Sample Outline – Speaker's Manual

The Canadian Society of Association Executives (CSAE)[10] prepares a concise and comprehensive manual for speakers at workshops and conferences. The following Table of Contents is from a manual used at a national conference.

Speaker Deliverables Checklist i

Welcome 1

CSAE Information 2

Program Flow 3

Session Information
- Developing Your Session 5
- Non-commercial Nature of Sessions 5
- Handout Material 5
- Room Set-up and Audio-Visual Equipment 5
- Session Attendance 6
- Participating in a Conference Call (with the co-ordinator) 6
- Speaker Ready Room and Session Rehearsal 6
- Session Introductions 6
- Help During Your Session 6
- Evaluations 6
- In Case of Emergency – Prior to Event 6
- Expense Reports 7

Developing Your Session
- Developing Your Session Outline 8
- Methods to Increase Learning and Enjoyment of Your Session 9
- Developing Your Visuals 9
- Presentation Tips and Cautions 10
- Adult Learning Insights 11

---

10. Canadian Society of Association Executives. Reprinted with permission.

Tool 7.8

What Speakers Need to Know Before They Present

1. What would you like my talk to accomplish?

2. How does my presentation fit within the session purpose and objectives? How could this presentation contribute to the session outcomes?

3. Why did you decide to invite me?

4. Who are the participants, e.g., experience in the topic area, demographics, academic background, expectations?

5. Given the purpose and expected outcomes, what is the most appropriate tone, e.g., challenging, inquiring, advocating, teaching, learning, discussive, motivating, exploratory, etc.?

6. How do I fit into the flow of the overall agenda? What will participants be doing before the presentation? During the presentation? What activities will people be engaged in after the presentation, e.g., small group discussions, plenary questions and answers, solo reflective task?

7. What are some sample questions that participants are likely to ask?

8. Would participants benefit from having print materials related to this presentation? If yes, what do you have in mind? If no, why not?

9. If I supply print materials, I will want to retain copyright as they are part of a chapter from a book in progress. I will also want to ensure that these handouts are restricted to participants in my session and are not reproduced in conference proceedings. Are you comfortable with this?

10. What is your policy on marketing? Is it OK for me to mention my book?

11. What challenges is your organization/community/group facing that this session could address? Are there other hot issues for participants in this session that I should know about?

12. Given the background and experience of people in this workshop, what can I expect to get out of the session?

13. Do you have any special concerns about this presentation in relation to your workshop purpose or agenda?

14. What would make this a wildly successful presentation from your perspective?

Tool 7.9
Outline for a Letter of Confirmation to Speakers

- Thank you for accepting the invitation to speak
- Confirm the presentation
- Outline the purpose of the workshop, the agenda, and how the presentation fits in
- Focus of the presentation
- Print materials for participants
- Participants: number, backgrounds, experience
- Workshop needs assessment
- Timing of presentations and discussions
- Workshop package
- Commercialism policy
- Other speakers
- Travel and accommodation
- Workshop report
- Contact information

Template 7.10
Letter of Confirmation to Speakers

TO: Keynote Speakers, Municipal Planning Evaluation Workshop

FROM: Chair, Workshop Planning Committee

DATE:

SUBJECT: Information about the workshop

I am writing to follow up on our recent phone conversation regarding your participation as a speaker at the upcoming Municipal Planning Evaluation Workshop to be held in (location) on (date) at the (venue).

On behalf of the Workshop Planning Committee, thank you for taking the time and energy to share your expertise with this group. We are delighted that you will be sharing your insights with this group.

The purpose of this letter is to confirm our discussions and ensure that you have the information you need for your presentation.

The attached preliminary agenda describes the workshop objectives and outlines how the two days will proceed. As we have discussed, the purpose of the workshop is for participants to learn about municipal planning evaluation from experts in Canada and around the world and to share ideas and experiences with Canadian colleagues in this area.

Preliminary responses by participants to a questionnaire sent out about a month ago indicate that they are interested in hearing about the experiences of presenters and how they can apply that information to their own situations as evaluators of municipal planning. As a result, participants would benefit from some basic contextual information regarding your own situation but would appreciate the majority of your presentation to focus on what they can learn from you in relation to their back home situations.

Print Materials for Participants

To facilitate learning and note taking, we are asking each presenter to provide either a copy of slides or overheads or a one page, very brief, point form outline of the presentation. These will be photocopied and distributed to meeting participants for reference and note-taking purposes just prior to each presentation.

As discussed, we would like to receive these materials by (date) through email, courier or disc so that we will have time to format and make copies prior to the workshop.

Participants

There will be about 75 participants at the workshop. The majority will have little or no experience with evaluation of municipal planning. Some will have considerable experience in this field. Not all participants will have reviewed our new Guide carefully; some will have been involved in municipality related evaluation and may have different views than those in the Guide.

When they registered for the workshop, participants were asked to complete a questionnaire to help us organize the agenda. A summary of these responses will be presented at the workshop. You will receive a draft of the key points in this summary about a week before the workshop.

Timing of Presentations and Discussions

As the agenda indicates, we have a full morning planned and would like to stay on time. I will provide you with five minute and two minute warnings during your presentation so that you can pace your concluding remarks accordingly. In past workshop evaluations participants have commented on how valuable the discussion period following a presentation is in terms of applying information to their own situations. As a result we have provided a generous time period for this interaction.

Workshop Package

Enclosed is the pre-workshop package that is being sent to participants, including a draft copy of Learning From Experience: Guide to Evaluating Planning in Municipalities. At registration participants will pick up name tags, a registration receipt and additional background information as required.

Marketing

The planning committee invites you to display any books or brochures you may have on our resource tables. Promotion of publications, products or services is not acceptable in any form during formal or social workshop events.

Other Speakers

Enclosed are articles representative of the work of each keynote speaker. This information should provide a sense of the perspectives you bring as the first three presenters at the workshop.

Travel and Accommodation

For information related to arrangements for travel and accommodation, please contact (name) at (number) or (email address).

Workshop Report

We will be taping your presentations and developing a brief summary for inclusion in the workshop report. You will have an opportunity to review, edit and approve the final version for the report.

Once again, thank you for agreeing to provide your expertise at this workshop. The Workshop Planning Committee is delighted that you will be present both as a speaker and in workshop sessions.

We will be in touch with you shortly with more information about the workshop, including a final agenda, AV support and timelines for pre-workshop materials. If you have any questions or concerns, please feel free to call me at (telephone number) in Canada or outside of Canada at (telephone number - collect) at your convenience.

Sincerely,

Chair, Workshop Planning Committee

Tool 7.11

Outline for Final Pre-Workshop Letter to Expert Speakers

- Time to confirm final arrangements
- Attachments:
    - purpose, assumptions and final agenda
    - list of key terms and acronyms related to this workshop
    - background documents that participants have been asked to review prior to this session.
- Timing considerations
    - when your presentation starts and finishes
    - who will give you a two minute warning
    - time allocated for discussion
- Workshop tasks related to your presentation
- What participants will be doing during your presentation
- What participants will be doing after your presentation
- Audiovisual support
- When to arrive at the workshop room; who will meet you
- Print materials related to your presentation and when they will be distributed to participants
- When copies of these materials are required for printing purposes
- Participants: final registration number; backgrounds of those participating; what they said in the pre-workshop questionnaire that relates to the presentation
- Thank you

Template 7.12
Final Pre-Workshop Letter to Expert Speakers

TO: Keynote Speakers, Consultation on Values and Principles for Health Care Resource Allocation

FROM: Workshop Facilitator, on behalf of the Workshop Planning Committee

DATE:

SUBJECT: Your presentation at next week's workshop

Now that we are about two weeks away from the Consultation on Values and Principles for Health Care Resource Allocation, we would like to confirm our discussions and ensure that you are comfortable with the arrangements for your presentations. Attached you will find:

- The purpose, assumptions and final agenda for this workshop

- List of key terms and acronyms related to this session

- Two background documents that participants have been asked to review prior to this session.

Timing

Please note that your presentation begins at 1:20 p.m. after a short introduction by the Chair of the session. (Chair's name) will be giving you a two minute warning so that you can complete your remarks at 2:00 p.m. We want to ensure 15 minutes for questions and answers.

Workshop Task Related to Your Presentation

Prior to your presentation, (name) will be asking participants to take notes on the following question:

> *What is our speaker's best advice to health professionals who need to make hard choices in relation to health care resources allocation?*

After your presentation, participants will be using their notes from your talk as a basis for small group work on a case study. A copy of the case study and related worksheet is attached.

Audiovisual Support

We will have a data projector set up and ready to go with your presentation on it. A microphone will also be provided. Please visit the workshop room just before lunch so that we can rehearse the set-up and ensure that you are comfortable with the arrangements.

Print Materials for Participants

To facilitate learning and note taking, we would like to provide either a copy of slides or a one page, very brief, point form outline of the presentation. These will be photocopied and distributed to participants for reference and note-taking purposes just prior to your presentation.

As discussed, we would like to have these materials from you by (date) so that we will have time to format and make copies prior to the workshop.

Participants

There will be about 70 physicians and staff from health care associations participating in the workshop. The majority will have some experience in decision making related to health care resource allocation but most will likely not have had a structured opportunity to explore values and principles in this area with colleagues.

Once again – many thanks for taking the time to speak with participants at this important session. I know they appreciate your commitment and enthusiasm in this area and are looking forward to your remarks.

Best regards,

(name)

Workshop Facilitator

C. Panel Presentations

Panels need special attention – it's very difficult to do them well. Many of the tips, tools and templates outlined for speakers in sections A and B of this chapter also apply to organizing panels. The following tips focus on the unique requirements of panels.

TIPS

✓ **Choose the topic** for the panel and develop an outline of questions you want addressed **prior to selecting the panelists**. This often happens in reverse, when committee members know who the experts are in a field and want them to participate. When the topic and presentation outline are done after the speakers are selected, the purpose and objectives of the session often take second place in importance.

> *Many panel presentations are sabotaged by poor panelists. Sometimes the culprit is a person so used to gathering all the attention as a keynote speaker that he speaks for 45 minutes instead of the agreed-upon ten minutes. On top of that, he grabs the microphone to answer all the questions. Other times the villain is a big-name executive or industry leader who is, to put it mildly, downright dull.*[11]

✓ To avoid duplication or overlap, send panel members' **presentation outlines to one another** ahead of time. Hold a teleconference with panel members two or three weeks before the workshop so that they can meet one another, discuss how they fit into the agenda, share perspectives and concerns, and confirm logistics.

✓ **Meet with panelists** prior to their presentations so that they can meet one another in person and work out any final considerations prior to their presentations.

✓ Choose **a moderator** who is comfortable with the topic area but doesn't have a strong bias. Make sure that she is skilled and experienced in her role.

---

11. Kaete, Margaret. "Perfect Panel Presentations" in *Training, Off-Site Meetings*: supplement to the July 1994 issue, p. 14.

METHOD TO MAGIC

Diagnostic: This workshop on how to develop productive partnerships between the government and the voluntary sector had 50 participants. The purpose was to share experiences and learn from one another for the benefit of future, collaborative government/voluntary sector projects.

Decisions: Participants were seated in half-rounds of six people facing the front.

A panel of four speakers kicked off the meeting, with each panelist addressing the following three key points:

- collaborative projects I have worked on
- one thing I know for sure about collaborative, government/ volunteer sector initiatives
- the perfect project: my vision.

Each speaker had ten minutes to present six overheads. Time was provided for questions after each presentation. During panel presentations and discussions, participants took notes on key characteristics of projects that work. After the presentation, each table of six participants created its own checklist of key characteristics for effective project management. Tables reported on their work in plenary and came to agreement on a final checklist to use as a template for rating their own projects.

It's great to know I can use this checklist in a meeting I'm having later this week. What a great take-away. And we agreed on the key characteristics so easily.

✓ Watch television **news anchors and talk show hosts for tips** on how to make a panel interesting and engaging. Ensure that your moderator is perceived to be objective, is well informed on the topic area, has met with panelists ahead of time and has come prepared with some questions of his own to start discussion.

Part II: Tips, Tools and Templates

- ✓ Develop **criteria for selecting panelists**, e.g.,
    - has considerable experience in the topic area
    - has an interesting perspective that is clearly related to the workshop purpose and will engage and challenge participants
    - is well informed about other perspectives in the topic area
    - is able to engage others in debate and entertain new ideas
    - is likely to be a colourful, interesting speaker
    - has good listening skills and can respond well to questions
    - will restrict comments to suggested time limit.
- ✓ Set up the room with panelists sitting in **comfortable chairs** that enable them to interact with one another, as well as with participants. Swivel chairs work well for this type of interaction.
- ✓ If you know one panelist you want and are having difficulty finding others, ask your confirmed panelist for **suggestions about others** in the field.
- ✓ If you pay your panelists, make sure that **compensation is equitable**, e.g., a standard fee plus travel and accommodation. Paying one panelist more than another for the same engagement raises ethical questions and may cause unnecessary tension among panelists.

Tool 7.13
Checklist for Conducting Panels

- Select panel members who provide different **perspectives** – both popular and less popular – on the topic under discussion. Ensure that panel members' perspectives and credibility are based on experience in the topic area.

- Provide **adequate time for questions and discussion**. In some workshops discussion time needs to be longer than presentation time; in others, it can be as little as one-third of the presentation time. Use your Workshop Diagnostic Framework (Chapter 2) to help you decide how much time is required for both presentations and discussion.

- Provide an opportunity for **panelists to meet each other** at least a week prior to the session, either in person or by teleconference to discuss the purpose and objectives of the session, the perspectives they will take, and to explore possible questions from participants.

- Provide panelists with a **copy of each other's presentations** prior to the workshop.

- Set up **panel seating** so that:
    - panelists have eye contact with the chair, each other and with participants
    - easy conversation among panelists is supported
    - panelists are physically comfortable, e.g., chairs are at the right height
    - the order of seating supports the flow of the agenda
    - panelists can see their slides being projected
    - panelists can be heard easily by everyone in the room.

- Ask the Moderator or Chair to review the **introductions provided** by panelists and to customize them to suit the tone, focus and amount of time available. Ensure that each introduction takes about the same amount of time and highlights the importance of the speaker in terms of the session outcomes.

- Ask an organizing committee member to sit in full view of the panel to provide **timing notices** to panel members as required.

D. Closing Remarks

Just as opening remarks set the tone for the beginning of a workshop, so closing comments set the tone for wrapping up the workshop process and moving into next steps. Effective closing speakers have the ability to conclude a workshop so that everyone's views are represented fairly and participants have confidence that action will be taken on commitments made.

TIPS

- ✓ Choose your closing speaker carefully based on the kind of **impact** you want this person to have. Do you want someone who:
    - Has the credibility to encourage future commitment?
    - Will take responsibility for next steps?
    - Can motivate participants to pursue further involvement with your organization?
    - Will provide a warm and heartfelt thank you to everyone involved?
    - Will talk about how the results of this workshop fit with other initiatives in the organization or sector?
    - Can provide an on-the-ground perspective or a global, big picture point of view?
    - Can engender confidence in how organizers and participants will follow through on commitments and decisions made during the session?

- ✓ If possible, choose your closing speaker(s) **before the workshop starts** and ask them to think throughout the workshop about what they would like to say that would summarize the workshop results and close the session.

- ✓ If you don't know the workshop participants, consider choosing your closing speaker(s) **half way through the workshop**. This timing enables you to select speaker(s) whom the group seems to respect and it provides the speaker(s) with an opportunity to think about what they want to say and to collect a couple of quotations during discussions.

- ✓ Ask your closing speaker if she would like to sit down with you to go through some **ideas as a starting point** for her remarks.

- ✓ Prepare a list of the **people to be thanked** so that no one is forgotten.

- ✓ Encourage your presenter to **speak from the heart** in a positive and constructive manner.

- ✓ **Meet with the closing speaker** and a member of the workshop planning committee during a break before the end of the workshop so that you can share ideas and make sure all key points are covered.

✓ After closing remarks, do the **housekeeping details**, e.g.,
 - ask participants to recycle supplies such as name badges, extra paper, folders, pens and pencils
 - remind people that the workshop report will be coming to them for review shortly and you have a short turnaround time for their feedback
 - ask participants to take extra copies of reports with them if they can distribute them elsewhere for good use
 - make arrangements for your local food bank to receive extra food and drinks
 - remind planning committee members about their debriefing meeting immediately following the workshop.

Tool 7.14
Outline for Closing Remarks

- Purpose and expected outcomes

- Something significant that happened in the workshop

- Next steps and commitments, e.g.,
    - personal responsibility for action or change
    - organizational responsibility for action or change
    - report production and distribution
    - follow-through: immediate, short term and long term.

- Thank yous, e.g.,
    - participants for their time and energy
    - organizers for their efficiency
    - planning committee for their experience and wisdom
    - volunteer facilitators for their process skills
    - consulting group for their insights and facilitation
    - hotel staff for their service
    - organizational partners for their commitment to collaborate.

- Reference or quotation, e.g.,
    - something that stood out during the workshop or a quotation from someone in the workshop.

TEMPLATE 7.15

CLOSING REMARKS

Speaker: Director of Marketing

PURPOSE AND EXPECTED OUTCOMES

- when we started this workshop this morning we said that our bottom line was to get some clear goals for the next 12 months
- we have done that and more: we have also developed a strategy for addressing related issues and we have four volunteers for monitoring and evaluation.

SOMETHING SIGNIFICANT THAT HAPPENED IN THE WORKSHOP

- I am greatly encouraged by how we worked together to achieve these outcomes: we were able to move quickly past our personal differences to take a big picture perspective
- this is not easy to do: it takes some letting go and some trust that we will address these other concerns later
- I have your list of concerns here and I'm looking forward to building on the momentum developed at this session to start resolving these items at our meeting tomorrow.

NEXT STEPS AND COMMITMENTS

- everyone in this room shares the responsibility for acting on our decisions here today
- I will talk to our Human Resources people tomorrow about an incentive system related to these goals for our team: they have already indicated that they are open to working something out for us
- we have set up monthly review meetings to check our progress on these items; after that, our four volunteers will be checking in through these meetings to revise and update our goals and keep us on track
- our facilitator will be providing us with a draft report tomorrow; she will distribute it to all of us for sign-off – please do that within 24 hours.

THANK YOUS

- first let's give ourselves a round of applause for the time and energy that we have all contributed to making this day a success
- thanks to (names) for doing all the organizational work that provided the wonderful location, food and audiovisual equipment
- thanks as well to our facilitator (name) for her sensitive and yet firm hand in enabling us to do this work, and to our small planning committee of (names) for their experience and wisdom
- we will show our appreciation to the resort staff through a letter and gratuity.

QUOTATION

- a participant said something at lunch today that stood out in my mind: "If we want to be a successful profit centre in this company, we have to market marketing. Let's keep this theme in mind in our day-to-day work. We need to ask ourselves regularly how we are marketing marketing when we do business both internally and externally."

Chapter 8

Handouts

★ ★

★ ★

Handouts

The best handouts engage, direct and support participants in a session – they are one of the most influential methods a facilitator or manager can use to enhance individuals' participation, productivity and learning. Participants often keep handouts for reference after a workshop and share them with colleagues. This potential for widespread distribution reinforces the positive consequences of well-designed handouts.

Handouts appear in several forms and formats and at various times before, during and after a workshop. For the most part, they are hard copy or electronic pages that support the achievement of expected outcomes. Some handouts are one-page worksheets that provide instructions for participants on how to do a small group task; others are glossaries or lists of acronyms that are included in a pre-session package; still others are brief reports summarizing pre-workshop questionnaires or focus groups.

This chapter addresses three main areas for the development of exemplary handouts:

A. Content

B. Design

C. Six Key Handouts.

A. Content

In a world where the quantity of emails, voice mails and paper is mushrooming, while the quality is diminishing, the workshop management challenge is to develop well targeted handouts in an attractive and user-friendly format that captures and sustains participants' interest.[1]

Depending on the results of the Workshop Diagnostic Framework, a handout has, in varying amounts, three types of content: Information, Instruction and Inspiration.

Informational content provides facts and other data that participants need to feel comfortable participating in a session, e.g., a list of organizations represented at the session, ranked status of competitors' sales, a glossary of key terms or acronyms, an historical chronology leading up to the session, minutes of the last meeting.

Inspirational content focuses on motivation and may include quotations, useful references, things to celebrate, past successes, projected opportunities, thank yous, a list of best practices, key information about what other similar, well-respected organizations are doing in an area.

Instructional content focuses on the steps that participants need to take to accomplish a task, e.g., first they brainstorm all the "supports" in their region; then they brainstorm all the drawbacks. Then they create an action plan that capitalizes on the strengths and addresses the drawbacks.

If you are creating a worksheet that will enable participants to prioritize key challenges, this handout will be focused mostly on instruction with some basic information to guide thinking and perhaps a line or two to motivate quality work.

---

1. Davenport, Thomas H. and John C. Beck. "Getting the Attention You Need", in *Harvard Business Review*, September-October 2000, p. 119.

If you are creating a one-page handout on decision making that will enable participants to build consensus in a conflicted situation, then the handout content will likely include a fairly balanced emphasis on the three-I's: information in the form of a definition of consensus; inspiration in the form of suggestions for how to address the interpersonal challenges involved in building a lasting consensus; and instructions for the steps involved in building agreement.

Following is another example of an evenly distributed three-I handout.

METHOD TO MAGIC

Diagnostic: When preparing for a career development session, you anticipate that group members might get frustrated trying to think of the right action words for the start of their goal statements.

Decisions: Develop a mini-glossary handout that lists a broad range of optional verbs for people to consider as the first word in their goal statements. (See Template 8.5)

When I was stuck for the right verb for my action statement, I just referred to the Glossary of Verbs and picked the one that seemed to work best for me. This really moved me along and I spent a lot less time than usual on wordsmithing.

Handouts serve a variety of purposes, depending on when they are distributed. Ask your organizing committee what handouts they think people would want before, during or after a workshop.

Pre-workshop handouts can:

- initiate expectations about a workshop's design and outcomes
- cue participants to the tenor of the session, e.g., serious, fun, intense, comprehensive
- communicate goals or anticipated outcomes
- provide an orientation to the workshop: its setting, the participants and the facilitator
- increase the comfort level of session attendees by reassuring them about workshop organization and design
- inform participants about how to prepare for the session, e.g., complete a reading, review a report or a summary of participants' learning needs, fill out a worksheet, bring a particular item.

In-workshop handouts can:

- orient people to the facility and its features
- guide individuals regarding their participation in the agenda, e.g., roles, behaviours
- provide direction for an activity outlined on a worksheet
- act as a resource or reference tool, e.g., a list of acronyms
- initiate periodic follow-up and support for the client or participants on the workshop's outcomes.

Post-workshop handouts can:

- provide an opportunity for feedback on the session
- confirm next steps and follow-through with participants
- act as a reference tool, e.g., for further reading and learning
- enable further contact among workshop participants
- enable participants to claim for travel and accommodation expenses

Sometimes the simplest handout can weave more magic than anticipated as described in the following example.

METHOD TO MAGIC

Diagnostic: People of different backgrounds, experience and/or expertise are attending the first National Alliance Meeting for Owners of Pets with Diabetes. Many have indicated that although they are proud to be invited, this is their first workshop experience and they are somewhat anxious about meeting so many new people. Several also mentioned that they are wondering whether they have much to contribute.

Decisions: Seat five participants at each round table. Create a short, simple worksheet with three questions for participants to complete on arrival and to share with their tables, e.g.,

- Name, where from, contact information, i.e., phone, email.
- What is one thing you know for sure about pets with diabetes?
- What projects, groups and clubs are you currently involved in related to pets with diabetes?

We got off to a great start at this meeting. It felt good to be able to describe my local project and club to the people at my table. And I picked up a few naturopathic ideas for my club members just by listening to the others during introductions. I discovered that I had some good ideas to share.

TIPS

✓ There is a **right number** of handouts for each workshop. Too many handouts can cause confusion, irritate participants, provide too much information and give the impression of too much control. Not enough handouts result in participants lacking required information or having a hard time muddling through a task that could have been laid out clearly in a worksheet.

Finding the right number of handouts for a session means taking into consideration the purpose of the handout, the length of the workshop, expected outcomes and a host of other factors such as participants' predisposition to using handouts, experience of the facilitator and number of people in the room.

✓ Check to ensure that **terminology is consistent** throughout various handouts for a workshop.

✓ **Distribute handouts efficiently** when their content is required so that the flow of the workshop is not disrupted, e.g., if there are six tables, stack the handouts in groups of six, or decide in advance what assistance you require for distribution.

✓ Include **references** for original materials, quotations and ideas, particularly when items are photocopied.

✓ Identify clearly any handouts that are **confidential or have restricted circulation**. Check at the end of the session to ensure that copies haven't been left on tables.

B. Design

When designing handouts, make decisions about format based on the goals you are trying to achieve in the workshop and the information you have collected in your Diagnostic Framework (see Chapter 2). Pay special attention to how the design of the handout reflects the type of session, the participants and the context.

TIPS

- ✓ Design **a simple, attractive common look** for handouts to be used in a workshop, e.g., using the organization's logo as a consistent theme. (Most logos can be downloaded from the Internet.) In collaborative workshops with more than one sponsor or involving a partnership, develop a design that accommodates the profile needs of all those involved.

- ✓ Choose **font types and sizes** based on readability, organizational norms and requirements and the climate you want to establish, e.g., formal, fun, academic. Consider participant demographics: are most people middle-aged and moving towards reading glasses? Be aware of special requirements for people with sight challenges, e.g., some participants may have trouble reading type on some colours of paper.

- ✓ Find out your **client's preferences** with respect to printing, e.g., on one or both sides of a page, plain or recycled stock.

- ✓ **Colour code** your handouts to enable easy identification during a session, e.g., a green agenda, a yellow list of acronyms, a blue glossary of key terms.

- ✓ When thinking about how to distribute and use handouts, take into consideration the professional or **organizational cultures** of participants. Sometimes participants from "high tech" cultures are uncomfortable with paper handouts and worksheets and prefer to use electronic work stations to get things done. Participants from other organizations may have opposite inclinations, particularly if they are uncomfortable using computers in workshops.

- ✓ Although some participants may prefer to receive packages **electronically** prior to a session, sometimes it is more efficient to send out **hard copies** that are organized and colour coded to enable participants to find a specific document quickly during a session. Also, electronic transmission frequently results in a variety of page breaks, resulting in confusing page numbers and packages that have the same content but look quite different.

- ✓ Design handouts that are accessible so that participants can **find information readily**, e.g., with headings and key steps outlined clearly, comparative charts that summarize comprehensive background data, enough space for recording responses, facts in point form wherever possible.

- During a workshop, avoid distributing handouts that are longer than one or two pages, particularly if they are written in paragraph form. Information written in this format is difficult to access quickly during discussions.
- When developing background information such as fact sheets, write in point form so that participants can find relevant information quickly.
- Consider providing participants with short summaries of documents in point form in hard copy while making the longer, more comprehensive background papers available on the Web through email links.

✓ Include **headers and footers** in handouts for easy identification of different documents. Consider the following options for what to include in headers and footers:

- page number
- name of section in a document
- title of workshop, name of session
- name of client or sponsoring organization
- special themes, e.g., you may want to include the organization's vision statement or a pertinent motto
- date that the document was finalized.

✓ Decide whether the **writer's (or consulting company's) name** should be included in the header or footer. If a client wants a report developed by an outside consulting company to be clearly identified as external to her organization, then she may want to have the consulting company's name given some profile in the document. On the other hand, if a document or handout was a team effort, or if the client wants the focus to be on her organization or a planning committee, it may be best not to have the writer's name in a prominent position.

✓ If you are hired to facilitate a session and are designing handouts, be clear about your values and ethics related to **marketing**. How comfortable are you about including your organization's name in a prominent position on handouts or reports that the client has paid you to develop and which legally belong to him?

> " *For most workshops, we prefer to highlight the client's name in the footer and maintain a lower profile for our company's name. This helps the organization take ownership for the workshop process and outcomes.* "

✓ As a **value-add**, provide additional take-home copies of handouts and worksheets so that participants can customize them for re-use in their own organizations.

> *" I always feel good when people request additional copies of a handout for their own use after the workshop. Then I know that what we have created has produced a little magic for participants. "*

✓ When making decisions about pre-session packages, think about the **needs and interests** of participants and clients:

- Is the package primarily for use during the workshop or will participants want to keep it for reference after the workshop is over?
- Will participants need to add pages or sections to the package during the workshop? If so, what is the quietest and most efficient approach for that purpose?
- How much time is available for distribution of packages? Will regular mail work or is a courier service required?
- How will packages be distributed? Binders, wire-bound and cerloxed documents need special protection to arrive intact and are usually sent by courier.
- Does the client have any discounted agreements with the postal service or courier companies?

✓ Most available hard copy packaging (such as cerlox and wire bindings, binders, folders and stapled pages) will work for **pre-session packages** and be customized with logos. The following tips are specific to their use in relation to workshops:

- **cerlox bindings** are handy for keeping information in tabbed sections; they tend to wear and crack over time; pages can't be inserted or removed easily
- **wire bindings** are also good organizers but tend to bend under pressure and then it's difficult to turn pages; pages can't be inserted or removed easily
- a **file folder** of loose leaf pages can be labelled to fit immediately into a filing system after the workshop; pages can be shipped conveniently, but it's easy to get disorganized unless headers and footers provide quick references and page numbers; if additional pages are handed out at the session it may be difficult to keep things in order
- **paper or plastic pocket folders** allow pages to be easily inserted and removed but the pockets don't usually hold a lot of information
- **ringed binders** are great for long-term storage and tabbed inserts keep things in order; they can be very noisy in sessions as people insert or remove pages but some of this interference can be controlled through the facilitator
- **stapled pages** work for small temporary groupings of information but may not be durable over the long term.

✓ Develop a list of **handout contingencies**, e.g.,
   - Bring an **electronic template** with you to a session so that if you need to create a worksheet quickly, you already have an appropriate design for getting started.
   - When travelling with luggage, keep **a master copy of your handouts in your carry-on baggage** as insurance against items being lost in transit.
   - At the end of a session, remove and **re-cycle** any workshop materials left in the room to ensure that confidential materials are disposed of or shredded.
   - Provide **blank mailing labels and large envelopes** on a back table so that participants can mail their workshop materials home if they prefer.
   - Bring **extra copies of pre-workshop materials** to the workshop to replace forgotten or misplaced packages.

Tool 8.1

Possible Handouts: A Checklist

Review the following alphabetical list and circle the numbers of handouts you want for your workshop.

1. Affiliated organizations and their interest in the workshop outcomes
2. Agenda: main sections, activities, timing, breaks, social events, resource people, keynote speakers
3. Area attractions of interest to participants during free time
4. Background reading, e.g., newspaper articles, papers, policies, historical overviews, statistical data, fact sheets, guiding principles, conceptual frameworks
5. Bibliography: references, further reading
6. Child care opportunities: who, what, when, where, how
7. Confidentiality agreement
8. Conflict of interest guidelines
9. Coupons for use in local restaurants, shops, art galleries, museums
10. Cover page for pre-session package: workshop title, date, location, client, host, sponsors
11. Feedback worksheets
12. Glossary: key terms, acronyms
13. Historical chronology: key steps leading up to the workshop
14. Implementation committee members: names, positions, coordinates
15. Information requested by participants during the workshop needs assessment
16. Invitation to special social event: time, date, location, information regarding a cash bar or appropriate dress
17. Key questions to think about before the workshop
18. Key stakeholders and a brief description of their stakes in the process
19. Maps and instructions, e.g., for walking tours, jogging paths, scenic attractions
20. Mission, vision and values statements
21. Organizational norms for workshops, e.g., promptness, quality of effort
22. Outlines of presentations, e.g., copies of overheads with places to take notes

23. Participants: name, organization, address, email, phone
24. Planning committee members: names, positions, coordinates
25. Purpose, objectives, expected outcomes
26. Questions to ask colleagues to prepare for the workshop
27. Recreation: location, schedule of activities
28. Related recent reports
29. Report on needs assessment, e.g., synthesis of interviews or questionnaires
30. Resource centre: list of items, hours when resource person present
31. Safety and security tips
32. Shuttle bus schedules to and from transportation centres and to other activities in the area
33. Small group membership
34. Souvenirs of the host city, region or country, e.g., pin, pen, small flag, sticker
35. Specialty items related to the workshop location, e.g., Canadian maple syrup, Texas beef, Paris nightclubs, wilderness photography
36. Sponsors: who is paying for what
37. Table of contents for a pre-session package
38. Technology tips: cell phone reception in the location, public phone access, computer hookups, advisory on tech etiquette, e.g., no cell phone or text messaging during the workshop
39. Tickets to events that the workshop is sponsoring
40. Travel and accommodation information
41. Worksheets: tasks to be done by participants during the workshop, e.g., introductions, priority setting, action planning, environmental scans
42. Workshop report: who will take notes, who will review draft report, when final version will be sent out and to whom.

Template 8.2

Introductions

Part One: In Plenary

1. Name, where from?
2. How are you involved in the area of this consultation?
3. What is one thing you would like to get out of this consultation?

Part Two: At Tables

4. What projects are you currently involved in or aware of that are related to the purpose of this consultation?

Project	Contact Person, Phone #

Please post this list of related projects on the wall in the space provided.

Template 8.3
Guidelines for Working Together

The following guidelines were mentioned by participants in pre-retreat interviews as being important for a successful retreat.

Put a (✓) next to the three guidelines that are the most important from your perspective.

    a. Keep the discussion on track.

    b. Caution each other about taking on too much.

    c. Confront key issues without being aggressive.

    d. Tap into all our talents, so we have energy and fun.

    e. Enjoy each other.

    f. Share the air time.

    g. Conduct one conversation at a time.

    h. Ask questions.

    i. Listen with your eyes, ears, head and heart.

    j. Start and end on time.

Are any key guidelines missing?

_____

_____

_____

TEMPLATE 8.4
RESOURCES FOR FURTHER LEARNING

Web Sites

Name	Address (url)

Books, Handbooks

IDSP Report No. 12, Report to the Workers' Compensation Board on Lung Cancer in HardRock Mining Industry, (date, location).

The Internal Responsiblity System in Regional Mines, (date, location).

Other:

_____

_____

_____

_____

Articles, Pamphlets

_____

_____

_____

_____

C. Six Key Handouts

Some handouts really work and make a significant difference to a workshop's success. It may take years of playing with ideas and observing a group's responses to fine-tune your handouts so that the content and format match participants' needs and enable them to achieve the workshop's outcomes.

One way to start creating new handouts is to develop them for situations where participants stumble, can't seem to catch on to an activity, or don't understand how to move forward. Out of this muddle you can create some magic. This section provides six favourite handouts that have generated bits of magic for participants:

Template 8.5 Glossary of Verbs

> Participants at planning retreats often wrestle with words when writing directions, goals, objectives and/or action steps. People with the best language skills are often the most comfortable and confident in these situations. Others get frustrated and suggest the group is "wordsmithing."
>
> *" Since developing the Glossary of Verbs handout, group members seem to laugh a lot more and are more efficient with their time. "*

Template 8.6 What are Mission and Vision Statements?

> In visioning sessions, participants often get confused about vision and mission. This handout helps address this problem. Sample statements within the client's sector are provided, so if you are working with a university, you can include other academic institutions' visions and missions.

Template 8.7 Quotables: An Introductory Activity

> Workshop introductory activities are most productive when they are developed with the context of the workshop's purpose in mind. This handout is designed to enable strangers' and/or colleagues' discussion of their insights on various perspectives of a workshop's purpose.

Template 8.8 Participant Information Bank

> In workshops where participants want more information about each other than is available on a name tag or in a basic participation list, create a participant information bank and distribute it electronically after the session. Categories in the bank are based on what participants want to know about each other.

Template 8.9 Program Information Bank

> In some workshops participants need specific types of information in order to collaborate with each other. This handout was designed to support collaboration among program coordinators working in similar areas.

Template 8.10 Acronyms Made Easy: Terms and Organizations

Participants in workshops often use acronyms as a verbal shorthand. Create a list of potential workshop acronyms to support communication and prevent people from feeling uninformed.

Template 8.5

Glossary of Verbs

The right verbs reflect your intentions about what you want to accomplish through your goals. Search through the following glossary and select the most appropriate verb for what you have in mind.

Change of Direction Verbs

Alleviate	Decrease	Expedite	Lessen	Reduce
Augment	Diminish	Expand	Lower	Strengthen
Accelerate	Direct	Extend	Optimize	Shorten
Adjust	Enlarge	Ignite	Prevent	Upgrade
Change	Eliminate	Improve	Raise	

Maintenance Verbs

Confirm	Keep	Monitor	Retain	Sustain
Continue	Maintain	Preserve	Reinforce	Stabilize
Emphasize	Manage	Protect	Support	Validate

Other Action Verbs

Advertise	Deliver	Enlist	Investigate	Produce
Analyze	Develop	Emphasize	Identify	Resurrect
Arrange	Define	Facilitate	Introduce	Recalibrate
Access	Distribute	Finalize	Implement	Review
Benchmark	Direct	Forecast	Incorporate	Stimulate
Coordinate	Determine	Formulate	Interpret	Schedule
Calculate	Design	Foster	Mobilize	Train
Consult	Draft	Harness	Measure	Update
Conduct	Enable	Invite	Organize	
Create	Enhance	Inform	Prepare	
Collaborate	Establish	Influence	Promote	

TEMPLATE 8.6
WHAT ARE MISSION AND VISION STATEMENTS?

	Mission	Vision
Communicates	Organization's purpose/function, clients, stakeholders, customers	The way the organization will be in the future
Time-frame	Present Current focus, e.g., up to one year	18 months to five years ahead Realistic stretch into a future state
Includes	What your organization does How you fulfill your function For whom you are in business Your value proposition, what makes you distinctive, unique	Where your organization intends to go — its preferred future An emotional pull that attracts people to identify with the organization and its mission A magnetic north that aligns diverse directions
Evolves from	Mandate Environmental scan Gap analysis Consultations with opinion leaders	Mission and mandate Environmental scan, staff and stakeholder experience Consultations with opinion leaders

Sample Short Mission and Vision Statements

	Mission	Vision
Regional Health Department	We excel at providing a diversity of health enhancing services that address growing and changing needs in our community	Leading the way to a healthier county
Car Rental Company	To ensure a stress-free rental experience by providing safe, dependable vehicles and special services designed to win customer loyalty	We will be recognized as the preeminent company in the rent-a-car industry in the areas of customer service and satisfaction; employee participation; return to shareholders
Disability Centre	To enable children and youth with disabilities and special needs to achieve their personal best	Defy disability
Automotive Retail Corporation	To be the best at what our customers value most	To be the first choice for Canadians in automotive, sports and leisure, and home products, providing total customer value through customer-driven service, focused assortments and competitive operations

TEMPLATE 8.7
QUOTABLES: AN INTRODUCTORY ACTIVITY

Solo Task

1. Following are four quotations related to the purpose of today's workshop.

    A. *Everyone thinks of changing the world, but no one thinks of changing himself.* (Leo Tolstoy)

    B. *Chaos is a friend of mine.* (Bob Dylan)

    C. *Change is an easy panacea. It takes character to stay in one place and be happy there.* (Elizabeth Dunn)

    D. *Don't agonize. Organize.* (Florence R. Kennedy)

    Rank these quotations according to what resonates most for you when you think about the purpose of today's workshop. (5 minutes)

Group Task

2. At your table, discuss the reasons behind each person's ranking of the quotations. In particular, note any curiosities or insights your group has about the similarities and differences among the rankings in relation to the purpose of this workshop. (1 minute per person; 10 minutes for group discussion)

3. In your group, develop your own "quotable" that reflects your group's insights.

Template 8.8
Participant Information Bank

First and last name: _____

Job title: _____ Base/Site: _____

Department: _____ Leisure Activities: _____

Discipline: _____

Phone number: _____ Fax: _____

Pager: _____ E-mail: _____

The number you call to book an appointment with me: _____

How you get referred to my services: _____

My areas of expertise: _____ Languages I speak: _____

Related teaching expertise: _____

What I am willing to share/provide, e.g., educational session on drugs, components of certificate program:

_____

_____

My pet project: _____

Educational background: _____

Affiliations: _____

Research in which I am involved: _____

Research trials: _____

Publications I would like people to know about (title, source, year):

_____

_____

Other information I think people would find it helpful to know about me:

_____

_____

Template 8.9
Program Information Bank

Program Name:	
Size of Full-time Staff: ☐ 3 or less ☐ 4-10 ☐ More than 10	
Our program is: ☐ Stand alone ☐ Integrated within a larger agency	
Contact Person: Email:	

Regional Characteristics:

- Population ☐ Rural ☐ Urban
- Language ☐ French ☐ English ☐ Spanish ☐ Multi
- Translation services available ☐ Yes ☐ No
- Serve First Nations, Inuit, Métis ☐ Yes ☐ No

Our program provides services for parents dealing with: (check any that apply)
- ☐ Developmental challenges
- ☐ Mental illness
- ☐ Substance use issues
- ☐ Involvement with the corrections system
- ☐ Child welfare protection
- ☐ Other

Our program is planning to provide services for parents dealing with: (check any that apply)
- ☐ Developmental challenges
- ☐ Mental illness
- ☐ Substance use issues
- ☐ Involvement with the corrections system
- ☐ Child welfare protection
- ☐ Other

Our program would like to access resource materials or mentoring on:

Our program can provide resource materials or mentoring on:

Template 8.10

Acronyms Made Easy: Terms and Organizations

ACE	Angiotensin-Converting Enzyme
ACES	Acute Coronary Events Surveillance System
ACHIC	Achieving Cardiovascular Health in Canada
ACHS	Federal/Provincial/Territorial (F/P/T) Advisory Committee on Health Services
ACPH	Advisory Committee on Population Health
ASCVD	Arteriosclerotic Cardiovascular Disease
BMI	Body Mass Index
BP	Blood Pressure
BRFSS	Behavioural Risk Factor Surveillance System

Chapter 9

Feedback

★★★★★★★★★★★★★★★★★★★★★★★

★★★★★★★★★★★★★★★★★★★★★★★

Feedback

Feedback happens in loops. The loop begins with a workshop. Then you gather and analyze information on the workshop from different perspectives. Then a summary report leads to informed decisions about what needs to be changed or maintained during future workshops, and in follow-up activities. The loop is closed when you act on the feedback.

Everyone connected with a workshop can provide feedback: participants, clients, sponsors, facilitators, managers, hosts, planning committee members, audiovisual technicians, caterers. This chapter focuses on participant feedback, and also provides reflective tools for clients and workshop managers.

This chapter has two main sections:

A. Getting Good Feedback

- What **information areas** do we want to explore?
- What **questions** will get us the information we want?
- What is the best **format** for asking those questions?

B. Acting on Feedback

This section emphasizes the importance of closing the feedback loop through implementation strategies.

A. Getting Good Feedback

Feedback is information that enables you to think about past experiences in terms of what you might want to do in the future in similar situations. Each workshop participant has her own perspective about the value of a session, depending on a complex mix of background, education, experience, personality and reasons for being involved. Gathering, understanding and summarizing a variety of perspectives on a workshop can provide valuable insights about what you need to do more of or less of, or to adjust or omit in future sessions.

You can access others' feedback by observing and clarifying body language, listening to comments and questions, or by asking questions yourself. For the purposes of this chapter, soliciting feedback is an efficient and fairly quick process.

Sometimes you can learn something significant by simply asking someone during a break, "So, how's the session working for you so far?" This type of formative feedback happens during a workshop: you check on how a session is progressing so that you can then make adjustments to ensure that the agenda is meeting participants' needs.

Summative feedback is usually more structured and happens after a workshop has concluded. It determines the workshop's value from a variety of perspectives such as participants', planning committee members', clients', sponsors', and organizers'. Summative feedback asks respondents to think about the nature of their total experience, often in the context of expected outcomes.

Sometimes, no matter how well-designed or intentioned your feedback mechanism is, you will get unanticipated or confusing responses, e.g.,

> Q: What are two things you liked most about the content of today's session?
>
> *A: The soft drinks at break. The washrooms were clean.*
>
> *A: Your smile and your hair.*
>
> Q: From your perspective, how successful were we in achieving our goals for this session?
>
> Insert scale of 1 - 5 (not successful to successful)
>
> Please explain your rating.
>
> *A: 1 - It was well done!*
>
> Q: One thing you think the company should follow up on after the Think Tank.
>
> *A: Give up while you're ahead.*
>
> Q: One thing you would like to change after this workshop?
>
> *A: Nothing, everything is fine with me. It's the person I report to who's the problem.*

Clearly, people may say what pops into their head first or makes them feel most comfortable no matter what the question! At other times your questions will solicit meaningful comments that enable decisions for generating magic.

METHOD TO MAGIC

Diagnostic: Your not-for-profit client group has scheduled their team-building retreat in a small, community centre that has seen better days but is provided free of charge. At the end of the first day of a two-day retreat participants are commenting on the poor air quality, uncomfortable chairs, cramped space, too few washrooms and noisy neighbours.

Decisions: You meet with the client and members of the organizing committee to discuss the feedback and explore options. A decision is made to stay put for Day Two and to take some steps to make things more comfortable.

The next day, you advise participants about the decision and rationale and ask for their input about what can be done to make this difficult situation more liveable. Participants use acceptance, humour and a few coping strategies to build a "can-do" spirit and their tolerance improves. Complaints are infrequent on the final evaluations.

I'm surprised at how we all worked together to turn a difficult situation into one that wasn't perfect but worked really well for us. I felt at one point that the challenging surroundings were just a tool that we could use as a team to address together. The fact that we responded to people's complaints went a long way towards making the session a success. We have some cool insider jokes now about that place.

1. What information areas do we want to explore?

Deciding what information to gather is a good place to start when developing feedback tools. Categories of information to consider include: satisfaction with the workshop; the quality of the learning experience; participation; application to the individual or organization; the workshop environment; logistics and organization; and next steps.

Different information areas vary in significance with different clients:

- When an under-funded school board chooses to host its planning day at the least expensive hotel they can find, having a high-quality, well-appointed workshop environment is obviously not at the top of their feedback list.

- When a well–established financial institution is hosting a one-time management retreat with surplus funds just prior to year-end, an enjoyable environment, recreational opportunities and appropriate logistical support may be more important in terms of feedback information areas than the quality of the learning experience or application back on the job.

- When people with physical disabilities are attending your workshop, access and the workshop environment are a high priority consideration in terms of feedback.

TIPS

✓ Review the areas that were identified as most important in the Diagnostic Framework (Chapter 2). Use these as a starting point for selecting feedback information areas.

✓ Connect the workshop objectives and expected outcomes to your feedback tools. When individuals can see that their responses will make a difference during or after the workshop, they will be more committed to investing time and energy to respond.

✓ Invite members of the organizing committee and the client to review draft feedback instruments. Will this get them the information they want about this workshop? How might they use this information after the workshop? What additional information areas would they like to explore?[1]

Use the tool on the next page to select information areas for feedback.

---

1. To read more about the messages inherent in evaluation, see Block, Peter. "How Am I Doing? How am I Really Doing? You Like Me! You Really Like Me!" in *The Flawless Consulting Fieldbook & Companion*, Peter Block (ed.) San Francisco: Jossey-Bass/Pfeiffer, 2001.

Tool 9.1

Areas for Feedback[2] Checklist

Feedback Information Areas	Participants	Client	Workshop Manager
1. Satisfaction with the workshop, e.g., Value of the workshop's activities and outcomes. Extent to which workshop goals/objectives were met. Reasons that explain any of the above, i.e., "why?"			
2. Learning experience and productivity, e.g., Extent to which the general workshop design and activities supported participants' learning. Outcomes such as team building, improved confidence. Adjustments that would have assisted participants' learning.			
3. Participation, e.g., Whether the right people attended the workshop. The effectiveness of individuals' participation in the group.			
4. The workshop environment, logistics, organization, e.g., Effectiveness of learning supports, e.g., facilitator, resource materials provided, location, wellness factors. Effectiveness of workshop advertising. Reasons that explain any of the above, i.e., "why?"			
5. Application and next steps, e.g., Type and extent of the workshop's impact on an individual's work life. Type and extent of impact on organization's bottom line.			

2. Donald Kirkpatrick provided the initial thinking on four levels of evaluation (see Further Reading).

2. What questions will get us the information we want?

Once you have determined the information areas, the next step is to develop questions for each area.

TIPS

- ✓ Make questions easy to understand by using **plain language.**[3]

- ✓ Start with **general questions first** and then move to more specific ones.

- ✓ To appeal to a range of thinking styles, include different **types of questions**: closed, open, multiple choice and scaled.[4]

- ✓ Focus questions on specific **things you can control**. If you can't do anything about what you are exploring, ask yourself if there is any point in inquiring about it.

- ✓ For written tools, limit the total number of questions to one or two pages – in general, **short is better than long**, particularly when respondents are tired or ready to leave.

- ✓ Keep the **pronoun consistent** throughout all questions: choose either "you" or "I," depending upon your preference.

- ✓ Forced choice questions can constrain or polarize thinking, e.g., Yes/No; Agree/Disagree. Rating scales invite respondents to **consider more possibilities** within a range of potential responses. This encourages valuing and discerning among gray areas, rather than contending with two opposites.

- ✓ For questions with **rating scales,** some evaluators prefer an odd-numbered range (e.g., 1 to 5) so that participants can respond with a middle ground of "3." Others prefer to encourage a response that does not sit in the middle and so provide an even-numbered range (e.g., 1 to 4). There is no right or wrong way to construct a scale – just be clear why you are choosing which scale, e.g., if you are working with a group that is indecisive, try a 4 point scale: it encourages people to make a decision that is not in the middle of the scale.

- ✓ The amount of **space provided** for an answer tells respondents how much information you are requesting. Don't provide three lines when you want three words.

- ✓ For **multiple choice questions**, list the possible answers and provide specific instructions such as: check only one, or check all that apply, or highlight only one.

- ✓ For the **final query**, encourage individuals to say whatever is important to them, e.g., *Other comments?*

---

3. To read more about plain english, visit the Plain English Campaign Web site at www.plainenglish.co.uk.

4. To learn more about asking questions, see: Strachan, Dorothy, *Questions That Work*. Ottawa: ST Press, 2001.

✓ Be sure that the tool reflects the **organization's culture**. If people say: *"We're very formal objective number crunchers and we take this quite seriously,"* or *"We're very laid back, fun and relaxed,"* how can you ensure that the tool matches the culture?

✓ Ask questions that enable the organizing committee to **anticipate post-workshop decisions** and actions that may be perceived as a threat or as an opportunity by different stakeholders.

Tool 9.2

Sample Questions for Information Areas

Once you have selected the categories of information desired, develop questions that will solicit specific information. Following are some examples.

1. **Overall satisfaction with the workshop**

    a. So far I would describe our session as: (circle one)

Unsuccessful				Successful
1	2	3	4	5

    b. Would you recommend this program to a friend?   Yes   No

    Please provide a reason: _____

    c. In your opinion, to what extent did we achieve the following goals of the session?

    _____

2. **Learning experience and productivity**

    a. One insight I had today was: _____

    b. What I found most/least useful about the session was: _____

    c. If you were the facilitator of the session:

    - What would you continue doing tomorrow? _____

    - What would you improve tomorrow? _____

3. **Participation**

    a. What I am learning from other participants: _____

    b. What we could do to help each other tomorrow: _____

    c. One thing I did to contribute to the success of the session:

    _____

4. **Workshop environment, logistics, organization**

   a. Please circle or shade the appropriate number to describe your opinion of the workshop setting:

	1 Poor	2	3	4 Excellent
General location, i.e., geographical location:	1	2	3	4
Workshop rooms:	1	2	3	4
Accommodation, i.e., hotel, community centre:	1	2	3	4
Food:	1	2	3	4
Ease of access:	1	2	3	4

   b. With respect to the workshop facilities and environment, I would like to say:
   _____

   c. What aspects of the facility or workshop environment:

      – Supported your learning? _____

      – Did not support your learning? _____

5. **Application and next steps**

   a. From your perspective, what is the most important factor affecting the success of _____ in following through on the session's action plan? Please suggest a way to address this factor.

      Factor: _____

      Action: _____

   b. What would you say are the next steps that you need to take in order to reinforce what you learned? _____

   c. What are two things you learned that you would like to incorporate in your work as a member of the senior team? _____

   d. What are your suggestions for further follow-up activities?
   _____

   e. When you think about your next meeting with this group, what would you include in the agenda? _____

   f. What concerns you most about the next steps? _____

3. What is the best format for asking questions?

The format of your feedback tool can influence the response you receive as much as the questions you ask. At the end of a long day, tired participants may be more responsive to three quick easy-to-read questions on one bright coloured page than to two white pages crammed with 15 challenging questions.

TIPS

- ✓ **Explore the benefits and drawbacks** of various approaches, e.g., benefits of verbal, written or electronic format.
    - Verbal: Quick, people hear each other's ideas and may piggyback on others' comments, energy (carefully weigh whether this could be positive or negative)
    - Written: Confidential, frees people up to say what is really on their minds
    - Electronic: Confidential, frees people up to say what is really on their minds.

- ✓ **Customize** your approach so that the format appeals to different types of participants in different types of sessions. At the end of a long session, some individuals are very stimulated and reflective. They prefer to write extensively about their observations when prompted by open-ended questions. Other participants are low on energy and prefer to circle a number quickly on a scaled question. Still others will ask: "Do we have to fill this out now? Can we send our responses tomorrow?"

- ✓ Consider ways to make the evaluation **attractive without biasing** the results in your favour. Clip art or a caricature of a bright light bulb may add an inviting but neutral look, while a light bulb with a smiling face on it may be perceived as inviting positive responses.

- ✓ Printing on brightly **coloured paper** enables participants to easily distinguish your instrument from the other papers that they have used during the workshop.

- ✓ If the instrument is more than one page, try some **encouragement** at the bottom of the first page with a stylized arrow and "only 3 questions left!"

- ✓ Include a sincere **"thank you"** at the end for the time, energy and insights people have contributed.

- ✓ When you want to **compare specific feedback results** over a number of sessions, keep those questions the same. Consider changing one or two other questions each session to get a variety of perspectives.

Tool 9.3

Designing a Feedback or Evaluation Instrument

Title: _____

Name of Workshop: _____

Date: _____

1. Provide a clear **introduction:**
   - How will the information be used? For example, read, summarized and acted upon, used to improve future sessions, used to enhance organization. Phrase it in a way that lets people know it is important.
   - Will it be anonymous and confidential?
   - Do you want them to provide names so that you can follow up on some aspect?
   - Who will get a copy of the results?

   Sometimes introductions are included on the feedback instrument and other times they are given verbally.

2. Choose the **information areas** that are most important to stakeholders – including yourself, e.g.,
   1. Satisfaction with the workshop
   2. Learning Experience or Productivity, e.g., planning session
   3. Participation
   4. Application and Next Steps
   5. Workshop Environment, Logistics and Organization.

3. Select the **questions** for each information area.

4. Provide **directions for returning** the completed tool.

B. Acting on Feedback

Although feedback has tremendous potential for insight and positive change, it is often just read and not used further. Completing the feedback loop involves listening actively to information received, summarizing it and using it to take action that will enhance the quality of future initiatives.

TIPS

- ✓ Provide participants with a **summary of feedback**. Be clear about possible changes for the future and how you and others will act on their suggestions. If you are using a formative feedback tool in the middle of a workshop, provide the feedback summary prior to moving into the next part of the session.

- ✓ Ask the organizing committee and/or client to **review an analysis of summative feedback results**. Discuss their suggestions about following through, e.g., what they might do differently next time.

- ✓ Set time aside to **reflect on feedback** as a strategy for continual improvement. Some workshop managers keep a journal of their reflections, reviewing them occasionally for recurring themes.

- ✓ Others **enter their reflections** into a database that automatically collates their ideas as each workshop is completed, generating interim reports.

    > *" It takes courage to be transparent about feedback. Sometimes when I'm picking up the feedback forms at the end of a session I just don't want to share them with anyone - especially when I see a "2" or "3" out of "5"- I start to feel discouraged and just want to go somewhere and hide. "*

- ✓ Compare the **summary of participant feedback** with: (a) your own reflections on a session (Templates 9.16 to 9.18) and (b) your client's feedback (Template 9.19).

Template 9.4
Interim Participant Feedback – A

Name of Workshop: _____

Date: _____

Please tell us how this session is working so far. Everyone's comments will be collated and presented back to the group for discussion and action. Thanks.

1. So far, I would describe our session as: (circle one)

   Unsuccessful   Successful

       1   2   3   4   5

2. What I like most about the session:

   _____
   _____
   _____

3. What I would like to see changed:

   _____
   _____
   _____

4. What I am learning from other participants:

   _____
   _____
   _____

5. Something else I'd like to say:

   _____
   _____
   _____

Template 9.5

Interim Participant Feedback – B

Workshop Barometer

Name of Workshop: _____ **Date:** _____

How is this session working so far? We will summarize your feedback and discuss it with the group. Thank you.

1. Right now I feel:
   _____
   _____

2. I probably feel this way because:
   _____
   _____

3. From my point of view, two of today's highlights were:
   _____
   _____

   Two of today's lowlights were:
   _____
   _____

4. A question or comment I had but did not raise is:
   _____
   _____

5. As far as our next session is concerned, I think:
   _____
   _____

Template 9.6
Interim Participant Feedback – C

Name of Workshop: _____ **Date:** _____

How is this session working so far? We will summarize your feedback and discuss it with the group.

Thinking about today's session, I feel (circle a face):

☺   😐   ☹

Why I chose this face:

_____
_____

1 insight I had today:

_____
_____

1 thing I wanted to say or ask today but didn't:

_____
_____

1 thing I liked the most about today's session:

_____
_____

1 thing I'd like adjusted for tomorrow:

_____
_____

Thank you

Template 9.7
Interim Participant Feedback – D

Name of Workshop: _____   **Date:** _____

How is this session working so far? We will summarize your feedback and discuss it with the group. Thank you.

What I found most useful about today's session:

_____
_____
_____

How I would describe the climate of today's session:

_____
_____
_____

What I would like our group to focus on in our next session:

_____
_____

What we could do to help each other maintain this focus:

_____
_____
_____

One other thing I would like to say:

_____
_____
_____

See you tomorrow. Please leave this sheet on your table.

TEMPLATE 9.8

DAY ONE FEEDBACK SHEET

Name of Workshop: _____ **Date:** _____

How is this session working so far? We will summarize your feedback and discuss it with the group.

1. If you were the facilitator of the session:

    – What would you continue doing tomorrow?

    _____
    _____

    – What would you improve for tomorrow?

    _____
    _____

2. On a scale of 1 to 5 how would you rate the session so far?

1	2	3	4	5
Poor				Excellent

    Reasons why?

    _____
    _____
    _____

3. What is one thing you did that contributed to your rating of the session?

    _____
    _____

4. What was not discussed that should be discussed before the workshop is over?

    _____
    _____

5. Other comments?

    _____
    _____

Thank you

TEMPLATE 9.9

END OF SESSION FEEDBACK – A

Name of Workshop: _____ **Date:** _____

We are revising this program. Please let us know what you think. Everyone's comments will be considered.

1. What did you want most out of this program when you signed up?
   _____

   Did you get what you wanted? _____ Please explain _____
   _____

2. What other things became important for you to learn while you were taking part in the program?
   _____
   _____

3. Overall, how well did you like the program?   (Circle a number)

1	2	3	4	5
Not at all				**Very Much**

   Please explain:
   _____
   _____

4. What did you like most about the sessions? _____
   _____

5. What did you like least about the sessions? _____
   _____

6. Would you recommend this program to a friend? _____ Why/why not? _____
   _____
   _____

Thank you

If you would like to get involved further with this program as a leader, or to assist with recruiting other leaders, please check : Yes _____ No _____

Name: _____ *(optional)*

Template 9.10
End of Session Feedback – B

Name of Workshop: _____ **Date:** _____

1. In your opinion, to what extent did we achieve the following goals of the module?

	1 Did not Achieve	2	3	4 Achieved
Goal #1: _____	1	2	3	4
Goal #2: _____	1	2	3	4
Goal #3: _____	1	2	3	4

2. What did you find most useful about the module?

3. What did you find least useful about this module?

4. If you were leading a module on this session, what is one thing you would do differently?

5. How will you describe this module to your colleagues?

6. Other comments:

Thank you for your participation

Template 9.11
Visioning Day Evaluation

Name of Workshop: _____ **Date:** _____

Please take the time to complete this evaluation and return it to us by email at _____ by _____. That will give us time to collate everyone's suggestions prior to the planning group's discussion of next steps. Thank you.

1. What did you find most worthwhile about the day?

   _____
   _____

2. What was not discussed today that you think this group should address at a future meeting?

   _____
   _____

3. If the day could happen again, what parts would you want to remain the same?

   _____
   _____

4. What parts would you want to see improved? How would you improve them?

   _____
   _____

5. What is one thing you did to contribute to the success of the session?

   _____
   _____

Template 9.12

Feedback on the Meeting

Name of Workshop: _____ **Date:** _____

1. The purpose of this meeting was to involve members of the X community in the development of a comprehensive network.

   How successful were we in achieving the meeting's purpose? (circle one)

Unsuccessful				Successful
1	2	3	4	5

2. What I appreciated most about this meeting was:

   _____
   _____
   _____
   _____

3. What I appreciated least about this meeting was:

   _____
   _____
   _____
   _____

4. Further comments:

   _____
   _____
   _____
   _____

   ...and Next Steps (please see reverse)

5. Would you/your organization like to be involved with the Network in the future?
   Yes ___ No ___

   If "no," please explain:

   _____

   _____

   If "yes," please indicate areas in which you would like to be involved, by checking the following appropriately:

   _____ Coordination   _____ Evaluation   _____ Content

   _____ Dissemination   _____ Operations

   How would you like to be involved?

   _____ As a member of a Working Group/ Committee, etc.

   _____ By receiving regular updates on the Network and its progress.

   _____ On an as-needed basis for the following areas of expertise:

   _____

   _____

   _____ Other (Please explain): _____

   _____

   _____

Thank you

Name: _____

Organization: _____

Template 9.13
Feedback on Planning Workshop

Name of Workshop: _____ **Date:** _____

Organization: _____

1. Overall, I would describe this workshop as: (circle one)

Unsuccessful				**Successful**
1	2	3	4	5

   Please explain your response:

   _____
   _____
   _____
   _____

2. From your perspective, what is the most important factor affecting the success of (organization X) in following through on the session's action plan? Please suggest a way to address this factor.

   Factor:

   _____
   _____

   Action:

   _____
   _____
   _____
   _____

3. Further comments:

   _____
   _____
   _____

Template 9.14
Conference Workshop Feedback Form[5]

Date: _____   Location: _____

I am evaluating (check one):

9am to 4pm   ___ Coaching Skills

9am to 12pm   ___ Understanding the Marketplace

1pm to 4pm   ___ Revenue Generation Options

                                ___ Group Facilitation: Asking the Right Questions

                                ___ Future Directions

Session Content

		Strongly Disagree		Neutral		Strongly Agree
a.	The session content was relevant to my needs.	1	2	3	4	5
b.	The session length was suitable to cover the content thoroughly.	1	2	3	4	5
c.	I learned valuable information/tools/ideas that I will implement in my office.	1	2	3	4	5

Presenter Effectiveness

a.	The presenter(s) delivered what was described in the session outline.	1	2	3	4	5
b.	The presenter(s) was engaging, interesting, informative and well prepared.	1	2	3	4	5
c.	The presenter(s) communicated effectively.	1	2	3	4	5
d.	The presenter(s) involved participants appropriately.	1	2	3	4	5
e.	The presenter(s) used appropriate audiovisual support.	1	2	3	4	5

Comments

_____

_____

Please turn in your completed form at the registration desk.

---

5. Adapted from a feedback form used by the Canadian Society of Association Executives.

Template 9.15

Feedback
Perspectives on a Symposium

The Perspectives Working Committee would appreciate it if you would take a few minutes to provide some feedback on this symposium. Please circle the appropriate number on the scale provided to indicate the degree to which you agree or disagree with the following statements.

		Strongly Disagree		Neutral		Strongly Agree
1.	Symposium objectives were realistic.	1	2	3	4	5
2.	Pre-workshop papers were very useful.	1	2	3	4	5
3.	Symposium registration was well organized, including travel and accommodation.	1	2	3	4	5
4.	Hotel accommodation/service was very good.	1	2	3	4	5
5.	Association staff were helpful and courteous.	1	2	3	4	5
6.	The facilitator enhanced the efficiency and effectiveness of the workshop.	1	2	3	4	5
7.	The general flow of the symposium agenda worked well.	1	2	3	4	5
8.	Overall, I would describe this symposium as a significant step in this consensus building process.	1	2	3	4	5

Additional comments:
_____
_____

9. What is one thing you and your organization/affiliation can do to continue the efforts begun at this workshop?
_____
_____

10. Further comments:
_____
_____

Thank you

TEMPLATE 9.16

WORKSHOP MANAGER'S REFLECTIONS ON A SESSION

Name of Workshop: _____ **Date:** _____

Session # _____

    Topics:

    _____

    Overall reactions to the session:

    _____

    What went well?

    _____

    _____

    Things I'd do differently if I could do it over again:

    _____

    _____

    Things I need to deal with in the next session that weren't completely handled in this one:

    _____

    _____

    What I learned as a facilitator:

    _____

    _____

    What I learned as a manager:

    _____

    _____

Template 9.17
Workshop Manager's Program Log – A

Program Dates:_____

Program Location: _____

Total time spent in preparation before the program started: _____

Review your session logs, thinking about the whole program.

- High points for you as a facilitator/manager:

  _____

  _____

  _____

- Low points for you as a facilitator/manager:

  _____

  _____

  _____

- What the group seemed to like most about the program:

  _____

  _____

  _____

- Things to note for the next time you do a program:

  _____

  _____

  _____

Template 9.18
Workshop Manager's Program Log – B

1. How did we do?	Not at All 1	2	3	Very Much 4	N/A
a. To what extent did our work assist the client in achieving their goals?	☐	☐	☐	☐	☐
b. To what extent did our work add value to the client's expected outcomes?	☐	☐	☐	☐	☐
c. To what extent did we deliver on time?	☐	☐	☐	☐	☐
d. To what extent did we deliver on budget?	☐	☐	☐	☐	☐
e. To what extent were client leaders engaged in the project?	☐	☐	☐	☐	☐
f. To what extent were we innovative on this project?	☐	☐	☐	☐	☐
g. To what extent is this innovative approach or product re-usable with other client groups?	☐	☐	☐	☐	☐
h. To what extent did we support positive visibility for our client among key stakeholder groups?	☐	☐	☐	☐	☐
i. To what extent did we enjoy this project?	☐	☐	☐	☐	☐

2. What difficulties did we encounter with this project?

   _____
   _____
   _____

   a. Did we contribute to any of these difficulties? If so, how?

      _____
      _____
      _____

   b. How did we help to resolve any difficulties?

      _____
      _____
      _____

3. What worked well?

   _____
   _____
   _____

4. If we could do this again, what would we do differently?

   _____
   _____
   _____

Template 9.19

Client Feedback

Feedback From You to Us

Please help us get better at what we do by providing some feedback on our work with you. You can return this page by:

    Email at: _____

    Fax to: _____

1. Overall, how satisfied are you with our services on this project?
   _____
   _____

2. What did we accomplish in this project that added the most value to your own or your organization's success?
   _____
   _____

3. What else could we have provided that would have been of assistance to you?
   _____
   _____

4. In one sentence, what will you tell your colleagues about our work with your organization?
   _____
   _____

5. May we use this statement as a testimonial when potential clients inquire about our services?   Yes ○   No ○

6. May we use your name as a reference when requested by future clients?
        Yes ○   No ○

Name: _____

Thank you

Further Reading

Anderson Fleming, Jean, Editor. *New Perspectives on Designing and Implementing Effective Workshops.* San Francisco: Jossey-Bass Inc., 1997.

Avery, Michel et al. *Building United Judgement: A Handbook for Consensus Decision Making.* Madison, WN: The Center for Conflict Resolution, 1981.

Block, Peter. "How Am I Doing? How am I Really Doing? You Like Me! You Really Like Me!" in *The Flawless Consulting Fieldbook & Companion*, Peter Block (ed.) San Francisco: Jossey-Bass/Pfeiffer, 2001.

Boud, David, and Virginia Griffin. *Appreciating Adults Learning: From the Learners' Perspective.* Toronto: OISE Press, 1987.

Bramley, Peter. *Evaluating Training Effectiveness: Translating Theory into Practice.* New York: McGraw-Hill, 1991.

Brookfield, Stephen. "Ethical Dilemmas in Evaluating Adult Education Programs." in *Ethical Issues in Adult Education*, Ralph G. Brockett. (ed.) New York: Teachers College Press, 1988.

Caffarella, R.S. *Planning Programs for Adult Learners: A Practical Guide for Educators, Trainers and Staff Developers.* San Francisco: Jossey-Bass, 1994.

Clarkson, M. *Taking Responsibility: The Ethical Imperatives of Stakeholder Management.* Centre for Social Performance and Ethics, Faculty of Management, University of Toronto.

Course Evaluations, Research Report No. 13. LERN Learning Resources Network, P.O. Box 1448 Manhattan, Kansas 66502, 1998.

Davie, Lynn. "Evolving Perspectives of Learning, Research and Programme Evaluation" in *Appreciating Adults Learning: From the Learners' Perspective*, David Boud and Virginia Griffin (eds.) London, England: Kogan Page, 1987.

Davie, Lynn E. "Program Evaluation for Instructors of Adults." in *The Craft of Teaching Adults*, Thelma Barer-Stein and James A. Draper. (eds.) Toronto: Culture Concepts, 1988.

Ellis, D. Reid, G. and Barnsley, J. *Keeping on Track: An Evaluation Guide for Community Groups.* Vancouver, B.C.: Women's Research Centre, 1990.

Gilmore, James H. and Pine (II), Joseph B. (Ed), *Markets of One: Creating Customer-unique Value through Mass Customization.* Boston MA: Harvard Business School Press, 2000.

Hiemstra, R. " Aspects of Effective Learning Environments." in R. Hiemstra (Ed.), *New Directions for Adult and Continuing Education No. 50. Creating Environments for Effective Adult Learning*, 41-50. San Francisco, CA: Jossey-Bass, 1991.

Hodgkinson, Christopher. *The Philosophy of Leadership.* Oxford, England: Basil Blackwell Publisher Limited, 1983. Of particular interest related to Chapter 1 in this book is the discussion of types on p. 138 – 139.

Justice, Thomas and David W. Jamieson. *The Facilitator's Fieldbook*. New York: HRD Press, 1999.

Kaete, Margaret. "Perfect Panel Presentations" in *Training, Off-Site Meetings*: supplement to the July 1994 issue, p. 11 - 16.

Kirkpatrick, Donald L. *Evaluating Training Programs: The Four Levels*. San Francisco: Berrett-Koelher, 1994.

Krein, T. and Weldon, K. "Making a Play for Training Evaluation" in *Training and Development*, April 1994, p. 62 - 67.

LaBarre, Polly. "Leader: Feargal Quinn" in *Fast Company Magazine*. Boston, MA: Fast Company, November 2001, p. 89 - 94.

Mackeracher, Dorothy. *Making Sense of Adult Learning*. Toronto: Culture Concepts, 1996.

MacLaurin, Dr. Don and Ted Wykes. *Meetings and Conventions: A Planning Guide*. Toronto: Meeting Professionals International, 1997.

Meeting Professionals International. *Meeting Manager Standards*. Mississauga, ON: Meeting Planners International, 1994.

Nolan Davis, Larry. *Planning, Conducting and Evaluating Workshops*. Austin, Texas: Learning Concepts, 1974.

Rodgers, Robert and John E. Hunter. "The Methodological War of the 'Hardheads' and 'Softheads'" in *Journal of Applied Behavioural Science*, Vol. 32 No. 2, June 1996, p. 189 - 208.

Scholtes, Peter R. *The Leader's Handbook: Making Things Happen, Getting Things Done*. New York: McGraw-Hill, 1998.

Schwarz, Roger M. *The Skilled Facilitator: Practical Wisdom for Developing Effective Groups*. San Francisco: Jossey-Bass Inc., 1994.

Senge, Peter et al. *The Fifth Discipline Fieldbook: Strategies and Tools for Building a Learning Organization*. New York: Doubleday, 1994.

Shenson, Howard L. *How to Develop and Promote Successful Seminars and Workshops*. Toronto: John Wiley & Sons, Inc., 1990.

Sork, Thomas, J. "Workshop Planning" in J. A. Fleming (Ed.), *New Directions for Adult and Continuing Education: No. 76. New Perspectives on Designing and Implementing Effective Workshops*, 5-17. San Francisco: Jossey-Bass, 1997.

Strachan, Dorothy. *Questions That Work: A Resource for Facilitators*. Ottawa: ST Press, 2001. www.stpress.ca.

Weaver, Richard G. and John D. Farrell. *Managers as Facilitators: A Practical Guide to Getting Things Done in a Changing Workplace*. San Franciso: Berrett-Koehler Publishers, Inc., 1997.